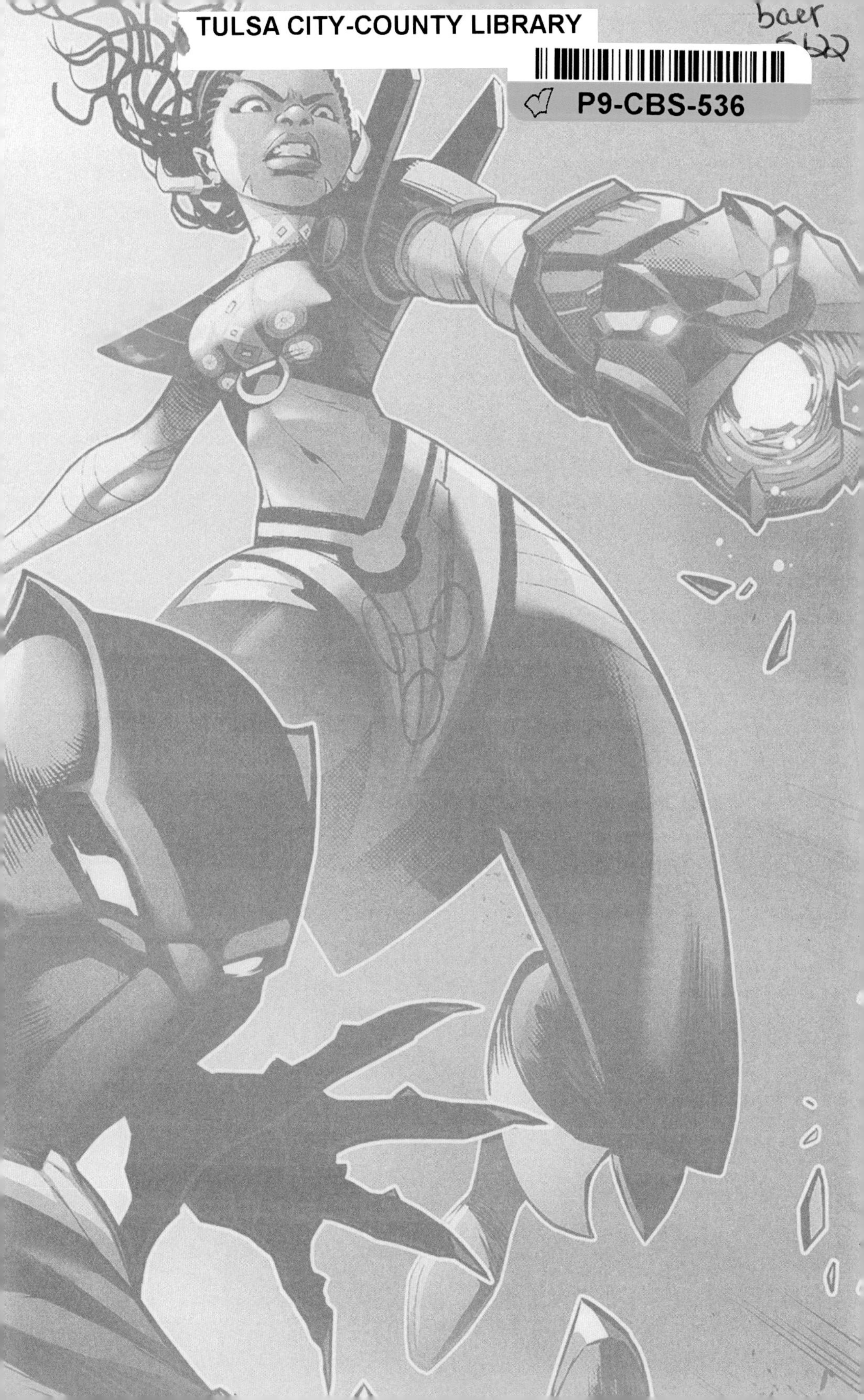

Penguin
Random
House

Project Editor Pamela Afram
Project Art Editor Chris Gould
Designer Ray Bryant
Senior Production Editor Jennifer Murray
Senior Production Controller Louise Minihane
Managing Editor Emma Grange
Managing Art Editor Vicky Short
Publishing Director Mark Searle

First American Edition, 2022
Published in the United States by DK Publishing
1450 Broadway, Suite 801, New York, NY 10118

DK, a Division of Penguin Random House LLC
21 22 23 24 25 10 9 8 7 6 5 4 3 2 1
001–326307–Jan/2022

©2022 MARVEL

A catalog record for this book is available from the Library of Congress.

ISBN 978-0-7440-4817-9 (Paperback)
ISBN 978-0-7440-4818-6 (Hardcover)

DK books are available at special discounts when purchased in bulk for sales promotions,
premiums, fund-raising, or educational use. For details, contact: DK Publishing Special Markets,
1450 Broadway, Suite 801, New York, NY 10118
SpecialSales@dk.com

Printed and bound in China

For the curious

www.dk.com

This book is made from
Forest Stewardship Council™
certified paper—one small
step in DK's commitment
to a sustainable future.

MARVEL
BLACK PANTHER

SHURI
DEFENDER OF WAKANDA

Written by Pamela Afram

Contents

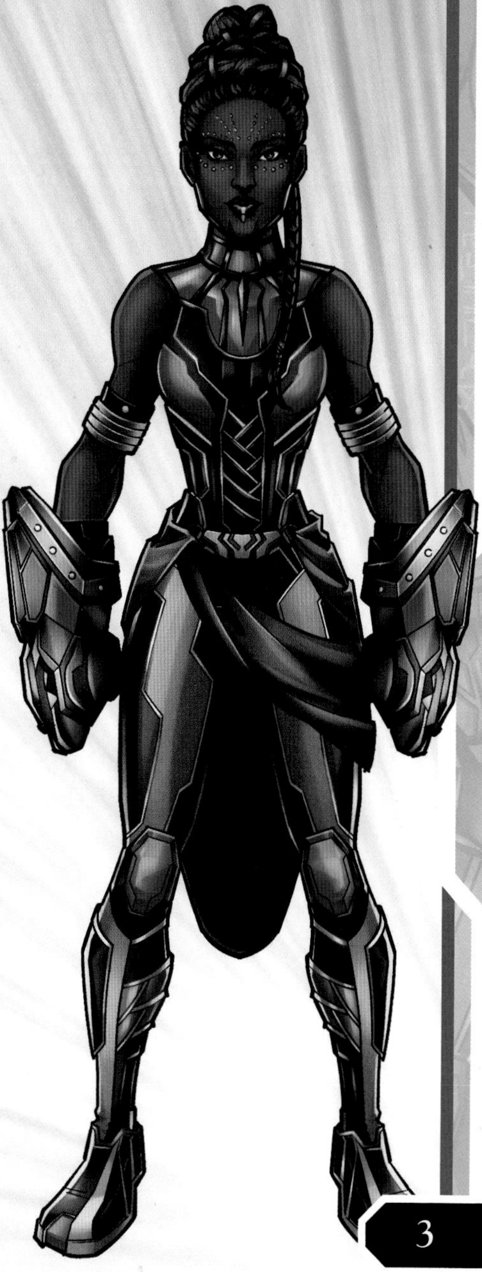

Mysterious Wakanda

Wakanda is an amazing place. It is the most scientifically advanced country in the world. The people who live in Wakanda keep their technology hidden from everyone. The rest of the world does not know how special Wakanda is.

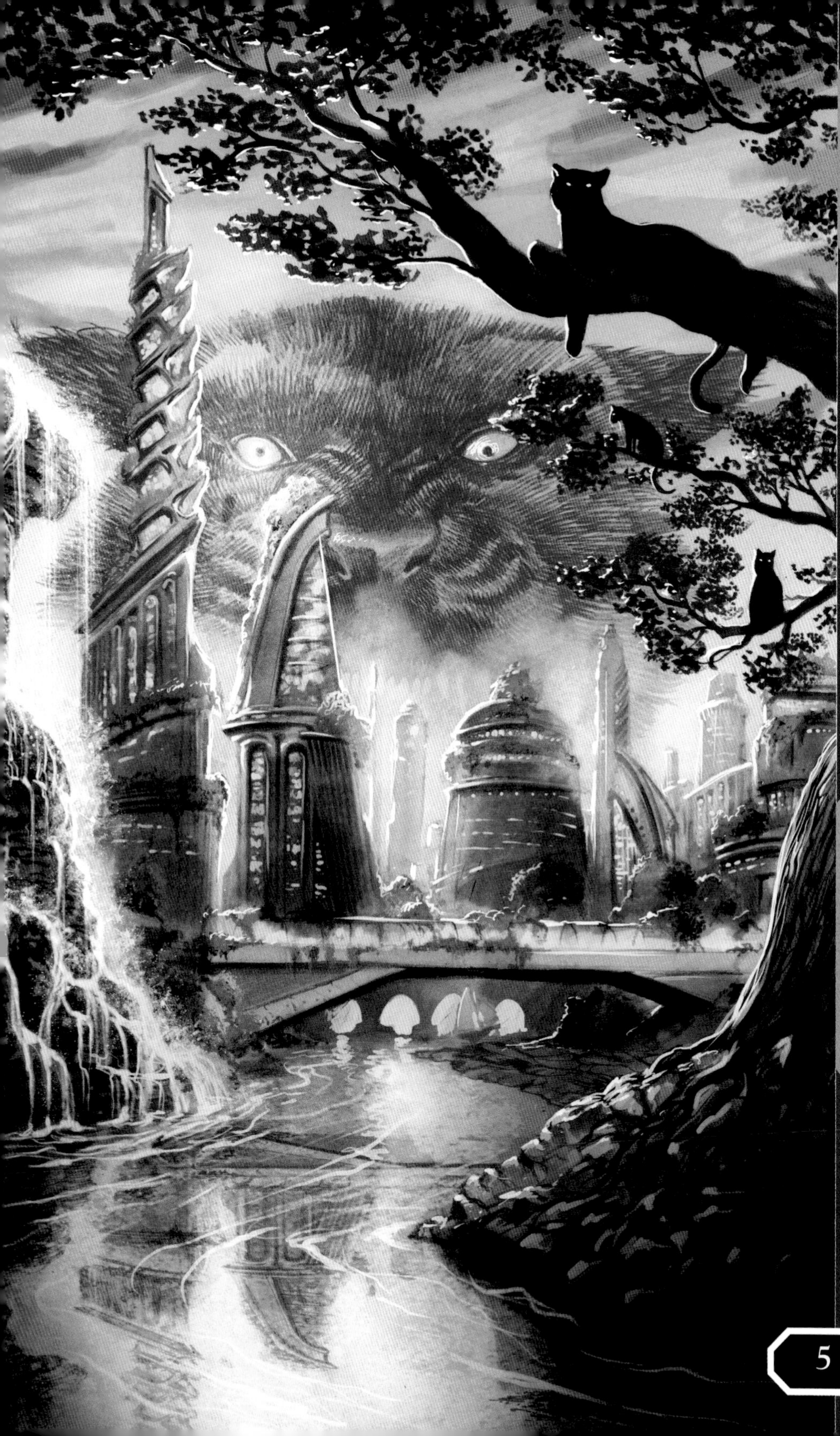

Vibranium

Ten thousand years ago, a meteorite crashed into an area of East Africa covered by dense forest. The meteorite contained a precious metal called Vibranium.

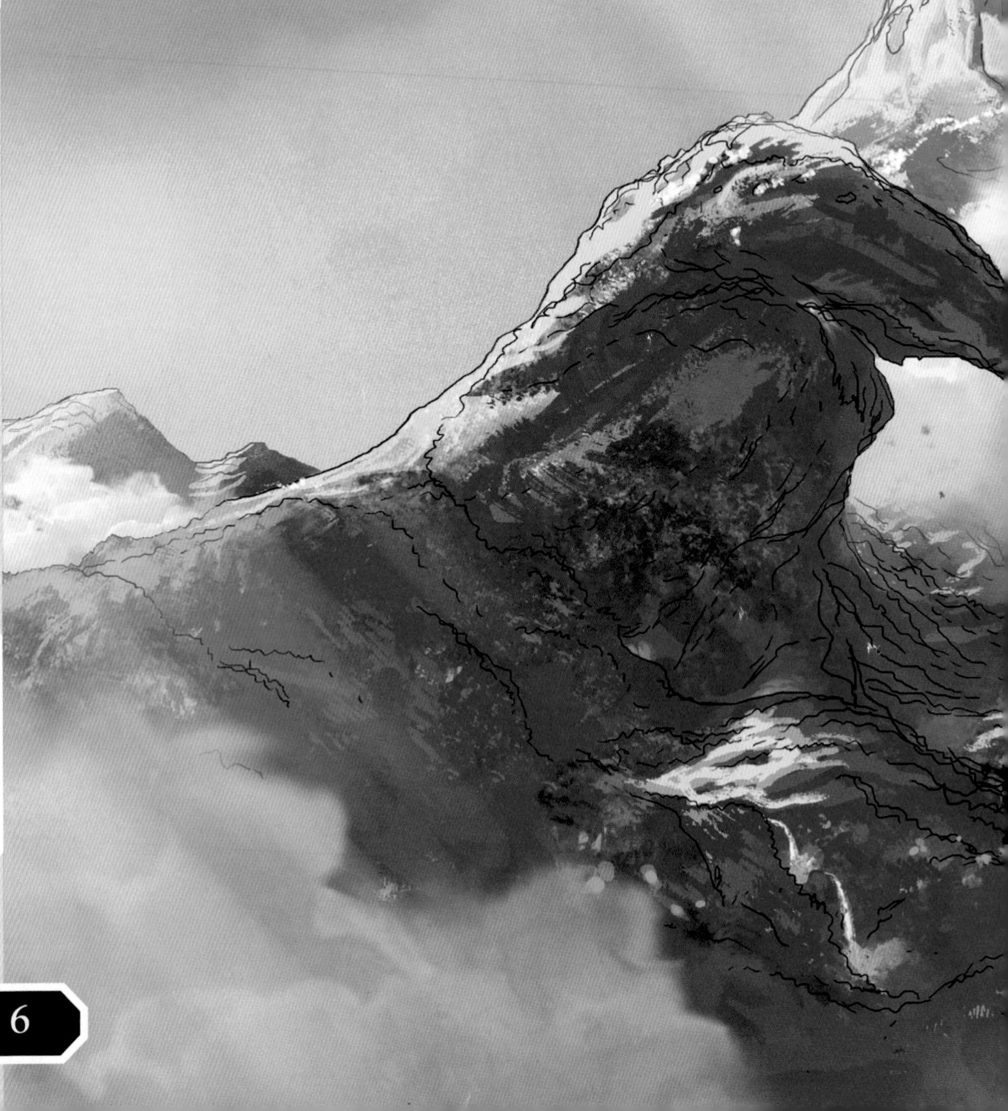

Soon after, people settled on the land and called it Wakanda. Wakandans use Vibranium to create their advanced technology and weapons.

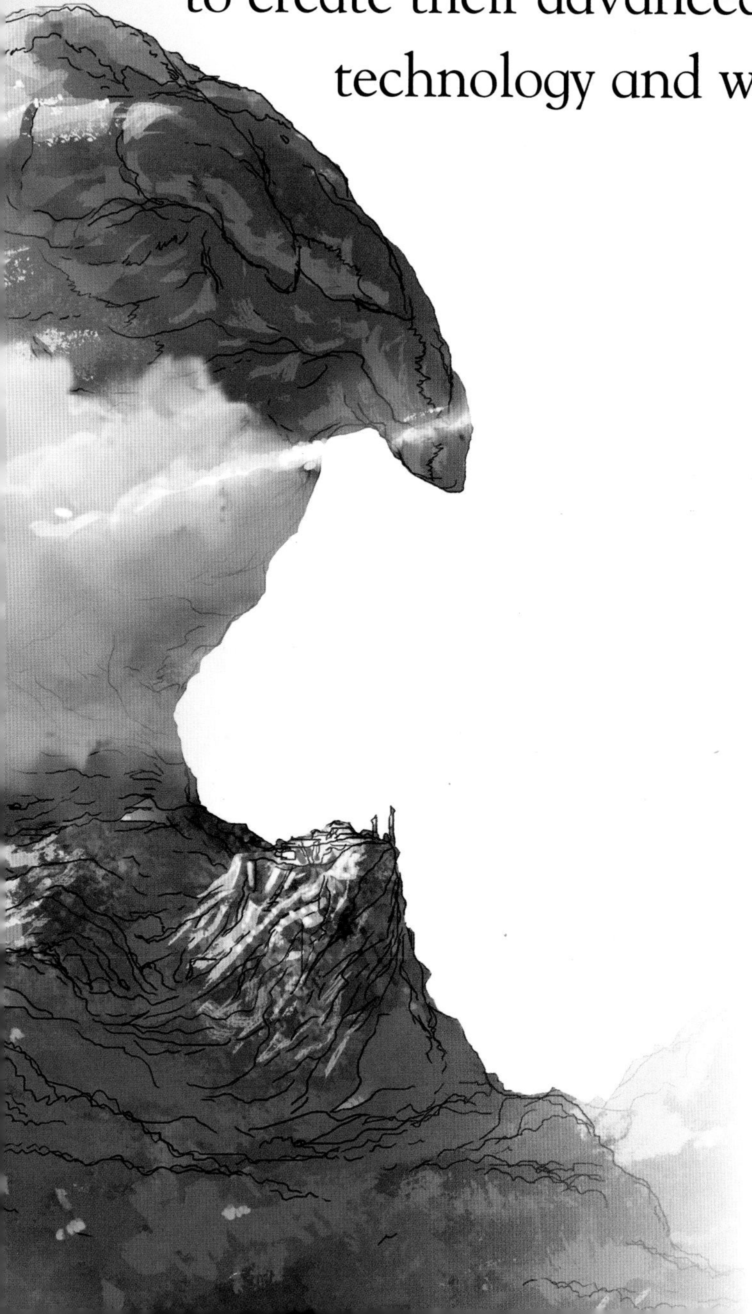

The royal family

Wakanda is ruled by King T'Challa. T'Challa has a younger sister named Shuri. Princess Shuri is the country's best scientist.

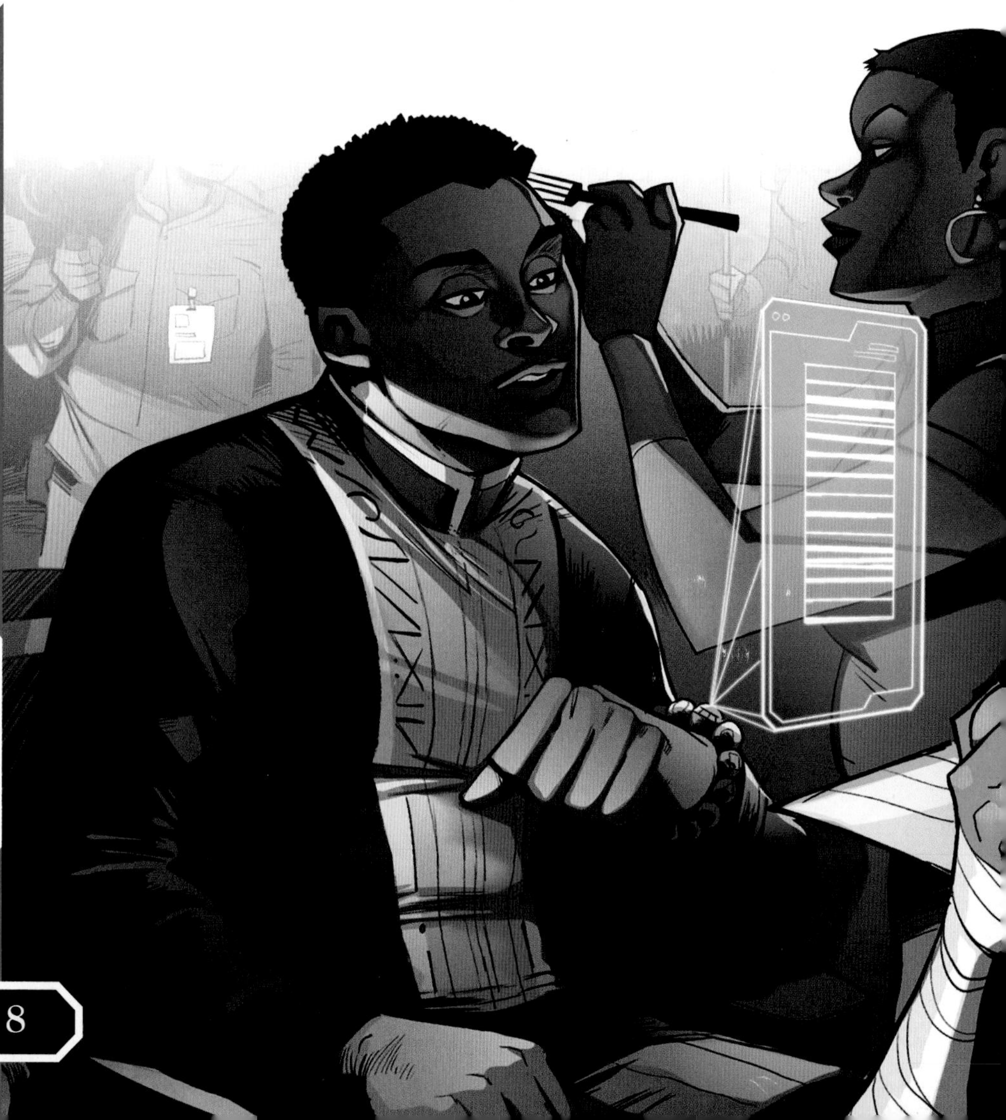

Shuri designs all of the amazing technology in Wakanda. T'Challa and Shuri are supported by Queen Mother Ramonda.

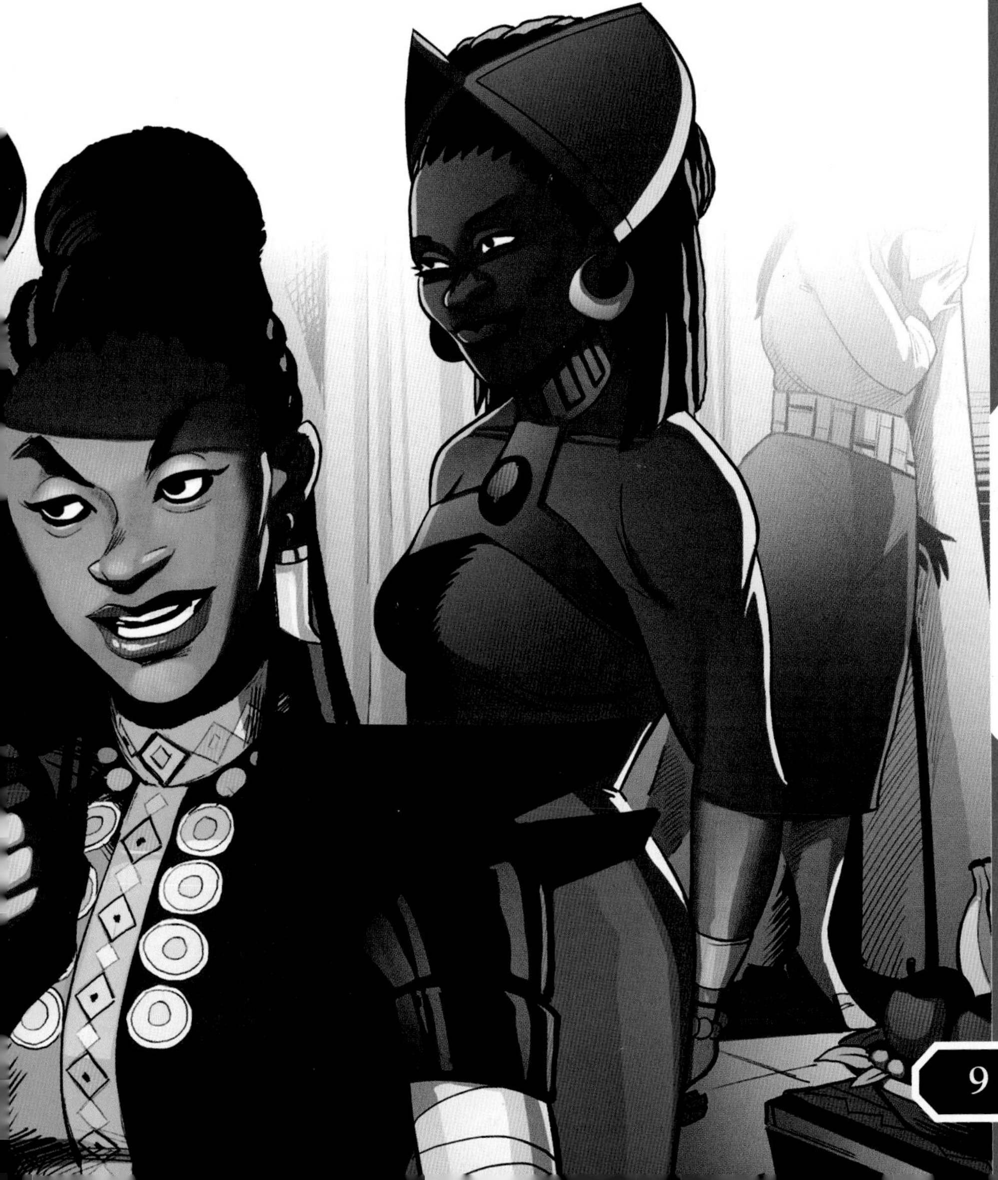

Shuri

Shuri is a genius. She loves science and inventing extraordinary gadgets and machinery. She spends most of her time in her laboratory.

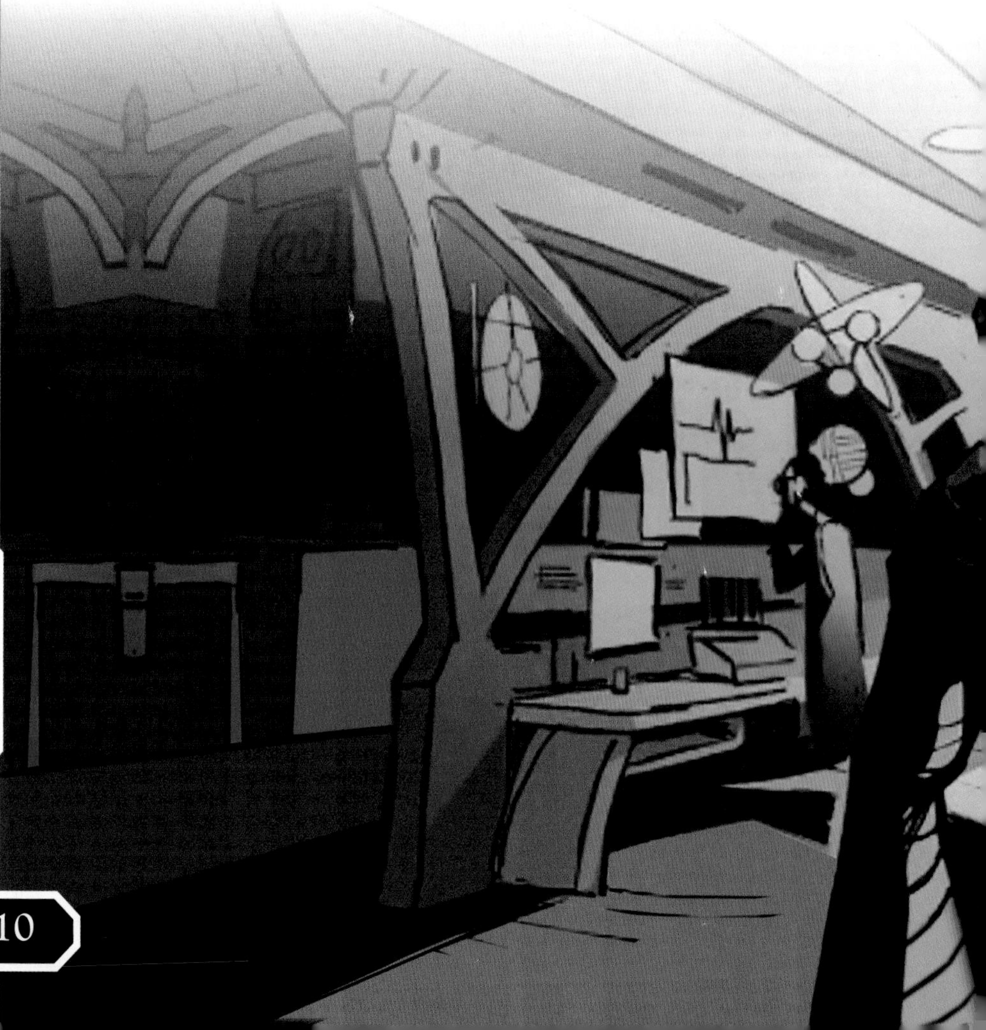

Shuri watches her brother closely. She has a lot to learn about being a leader. Shuri is heir to the throne of Wakanda and could one day be crowned queen!

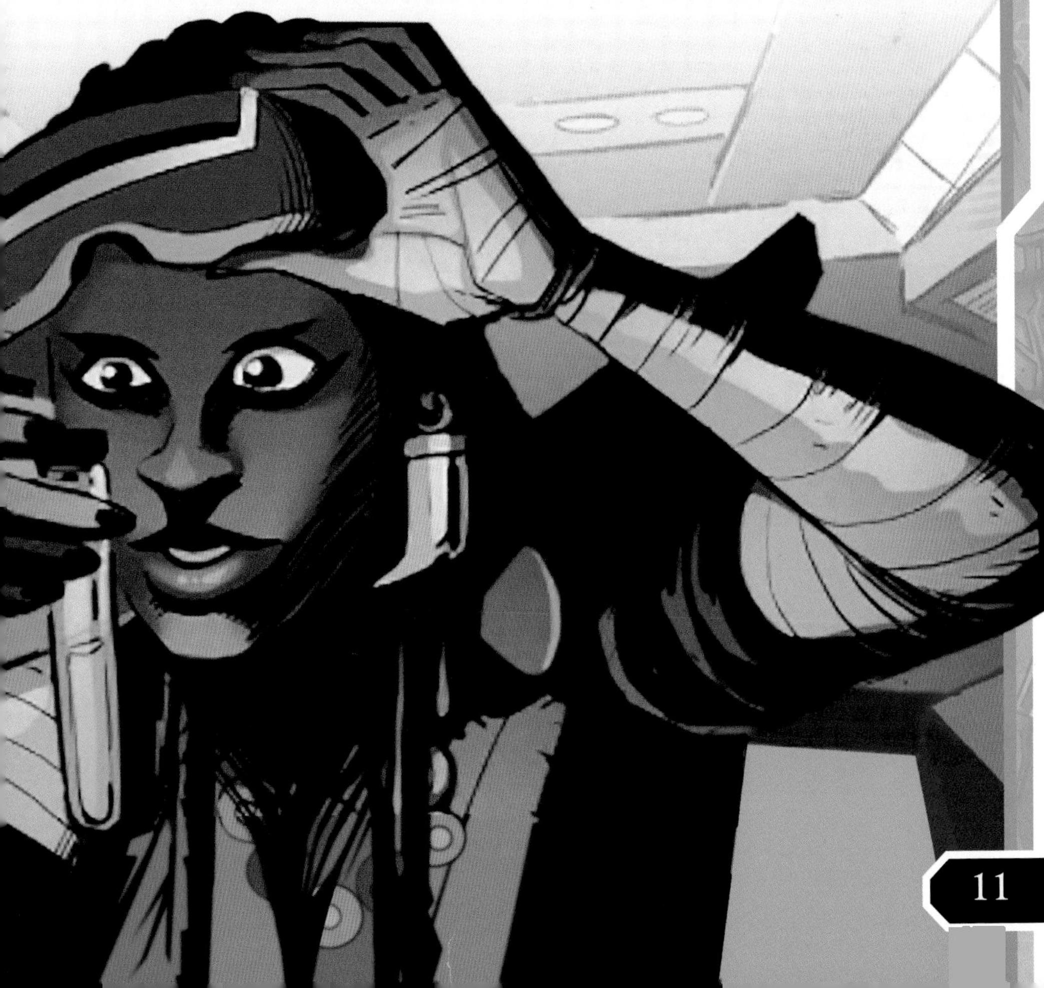

Super technology

Scientists have created remarkable machines and gadgets with Vibranium. This precious metal can make aircraft fly faster and even help people to communicate.

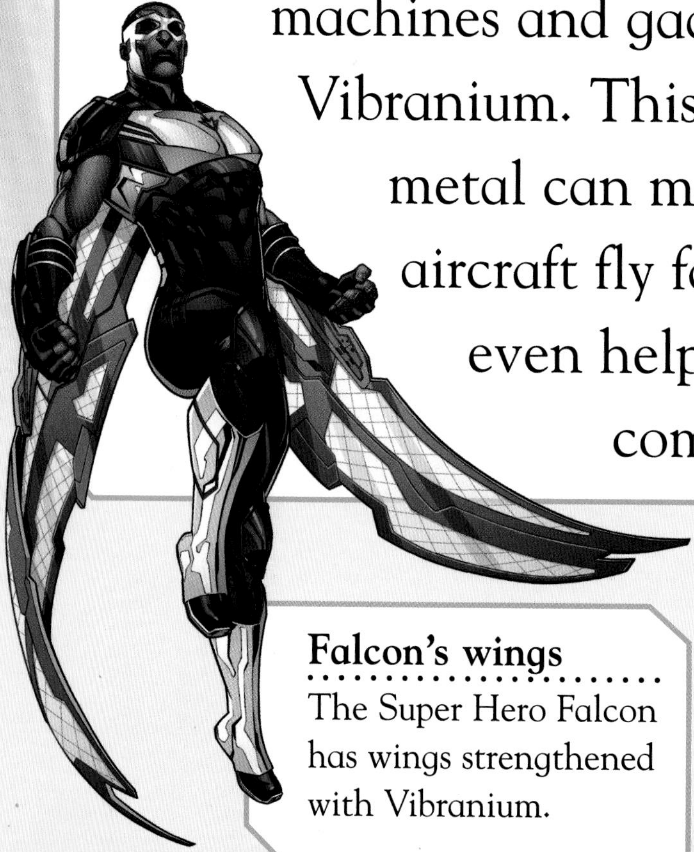

Falcon's wings

The Super Hero Falcon has wings strengthened with Vibranium.

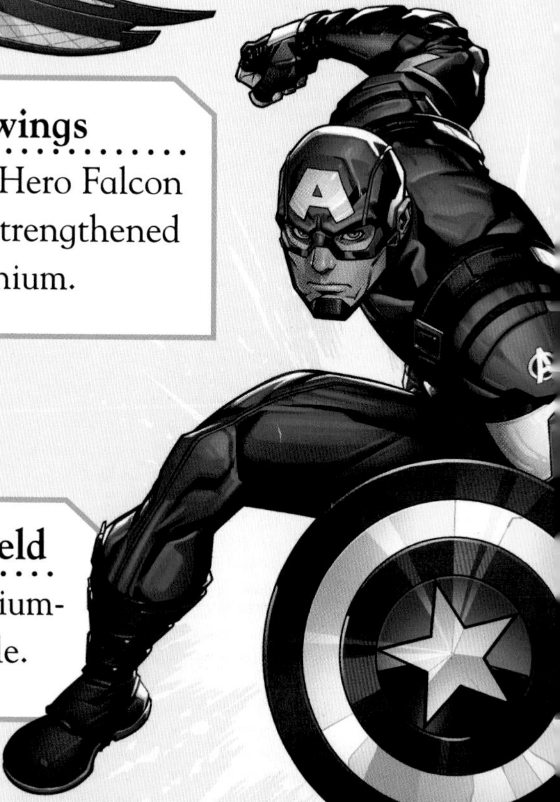

Captain America's shield

Captain America's Vibranium-filled shield is indestructible.

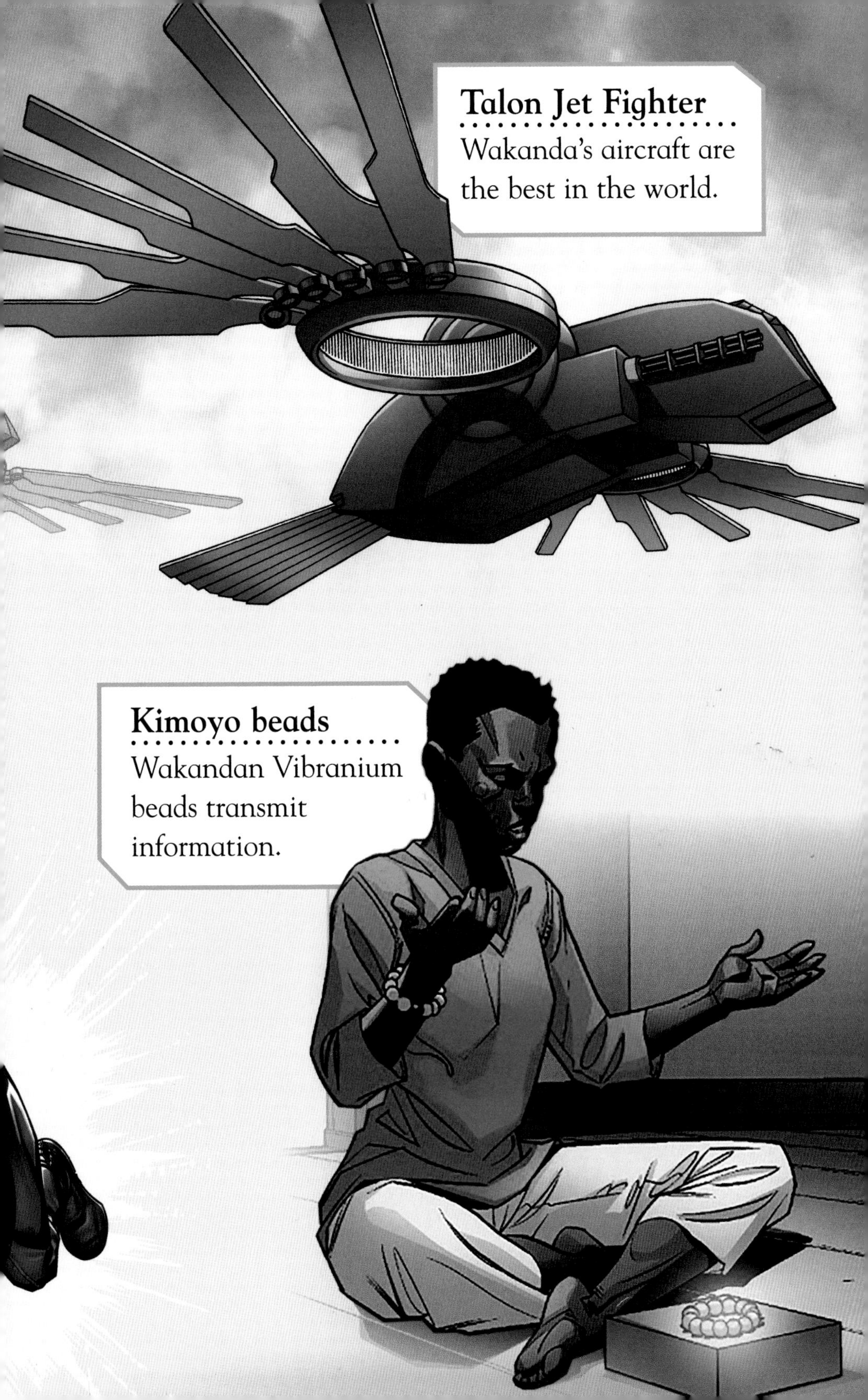

Talon Jet Fighter

Wakanda's aircraft are the best in the world.

Kimoyo beads

Wakandan Vibranium beads transmit information.

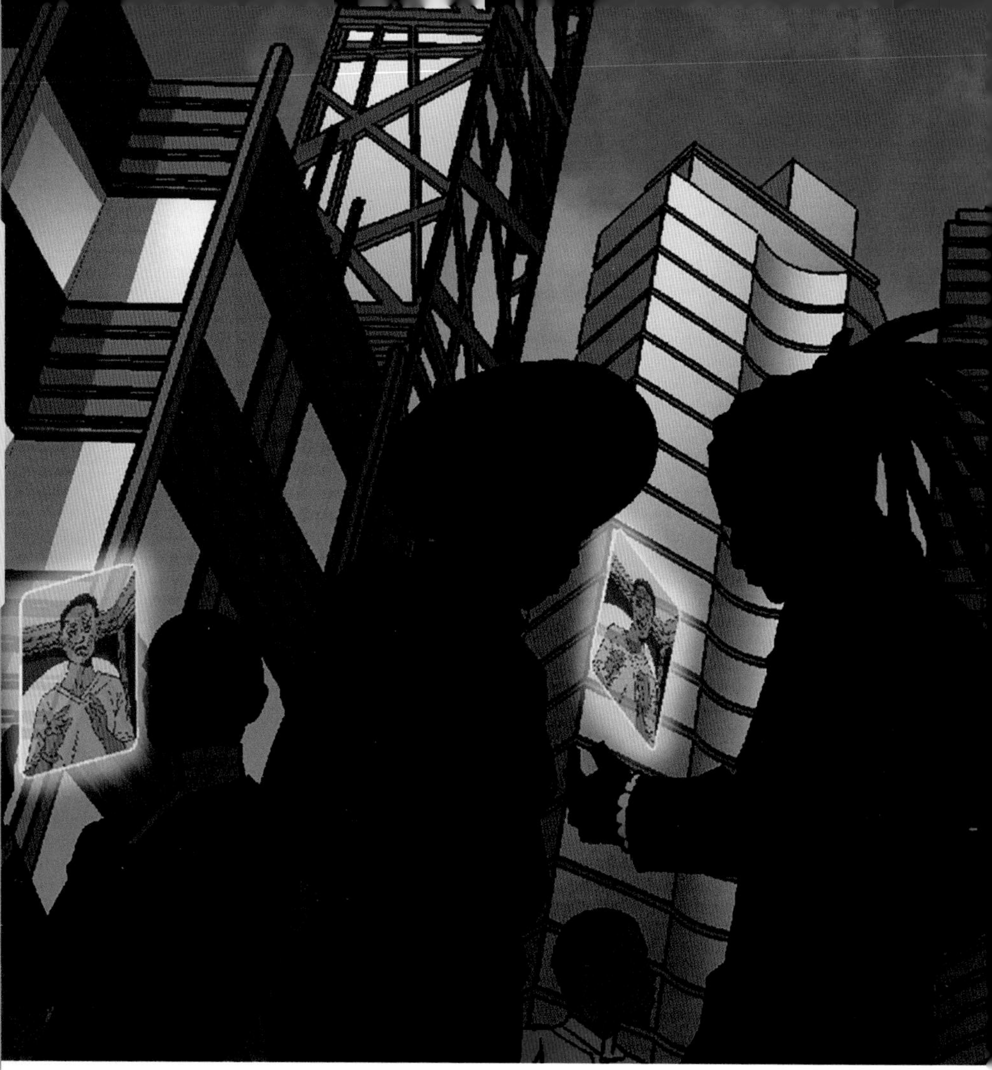

Birnin Zana

Wakanda's capital city is called Birnin Zana, or the "Golden City." The city is a dazzling place. It has lots of tall trees and beautiful plants.

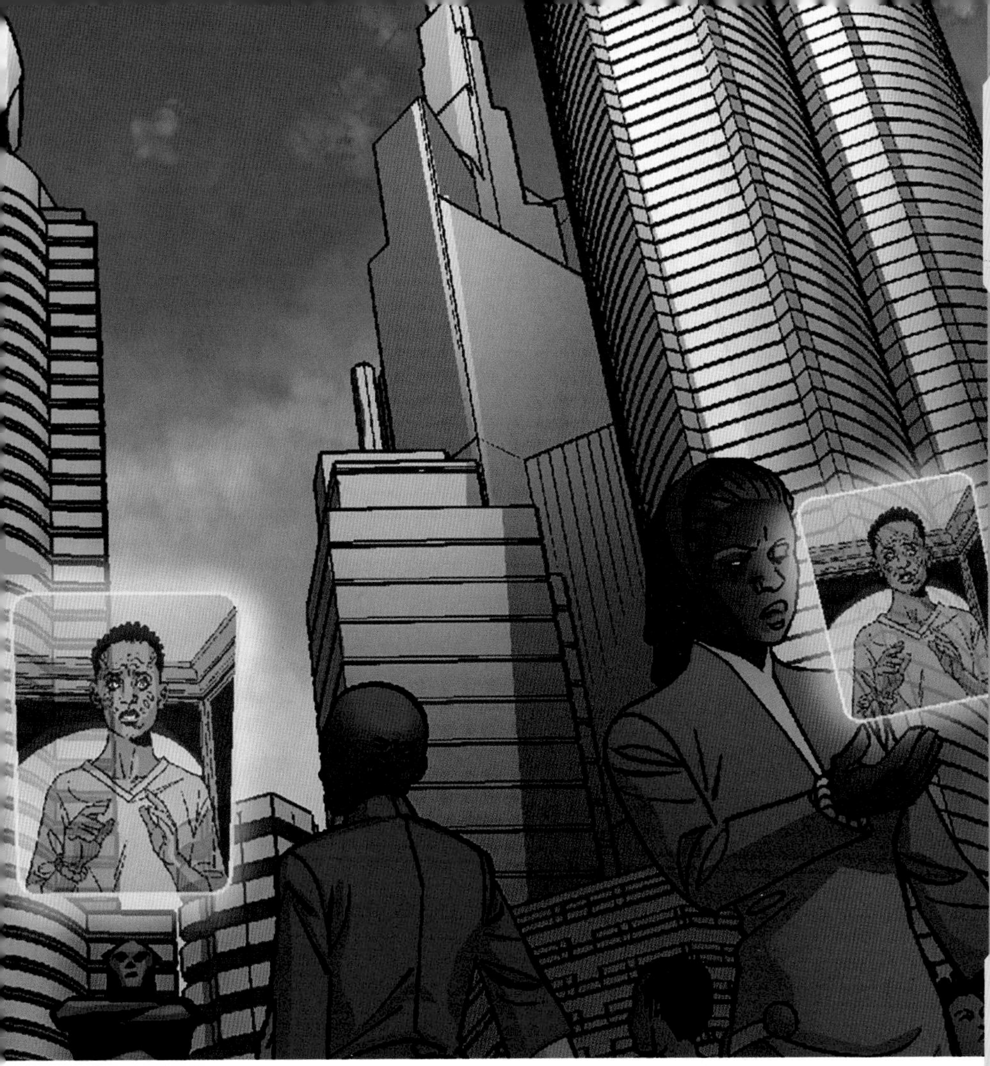

Birnin Zana also has gleaming towers and floating walkways. People travel around on a high-speed magnetic railway that runs through the city.

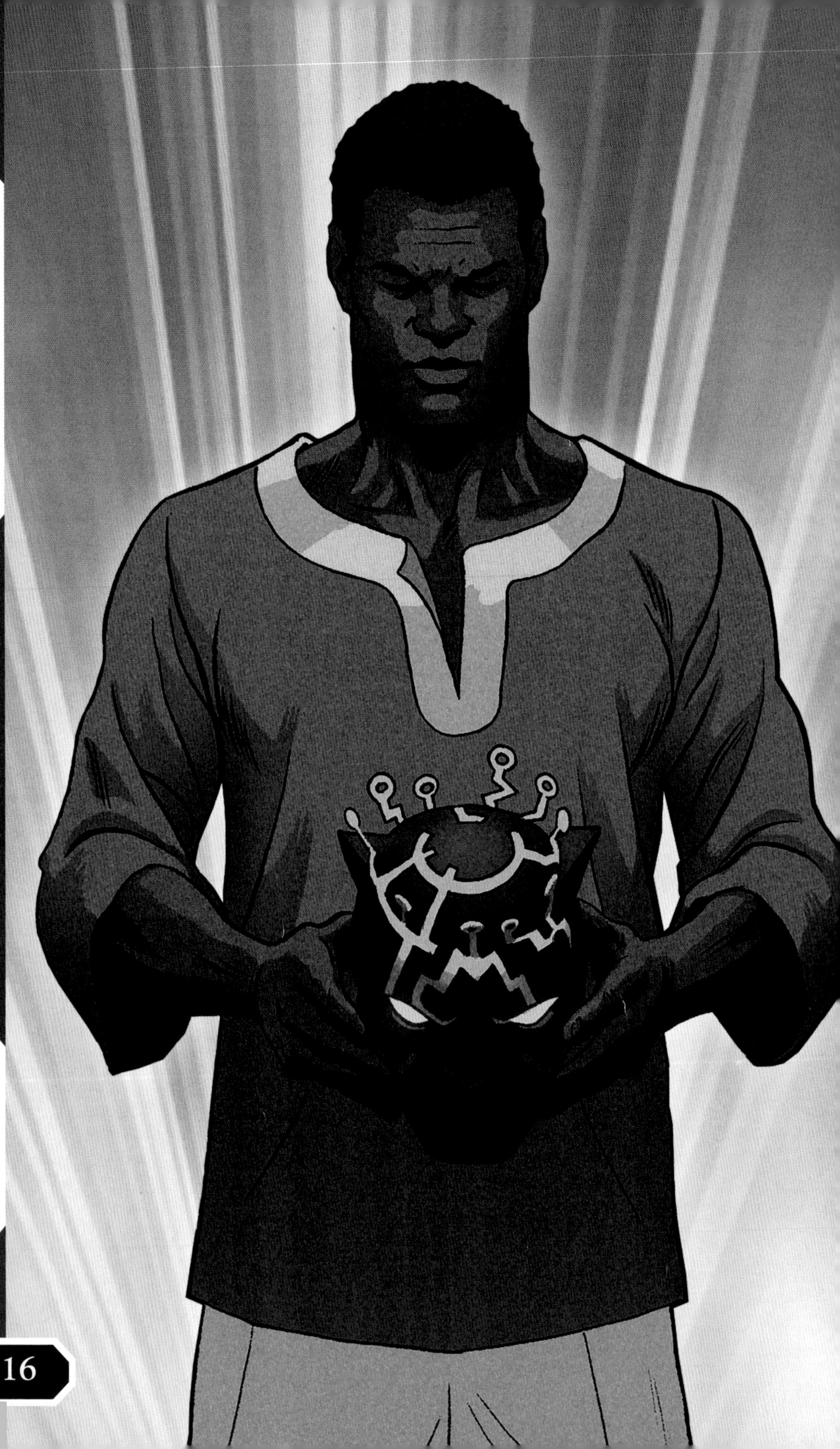

T'Challa

T'Challa is the King of Wakanda. He is a kind and strong leader who only wants the best for Wakanda and its people. Whenever Wakanda is under threat, T'Challa puts on a panther mask and becomes the powerful Super Hero Black Panther.

Honor and duty

A Black Panther must be kind, strong, and clever. Black Panther has a duty to protect Wakanda's technology and Vibranium from those who wish to do harm.

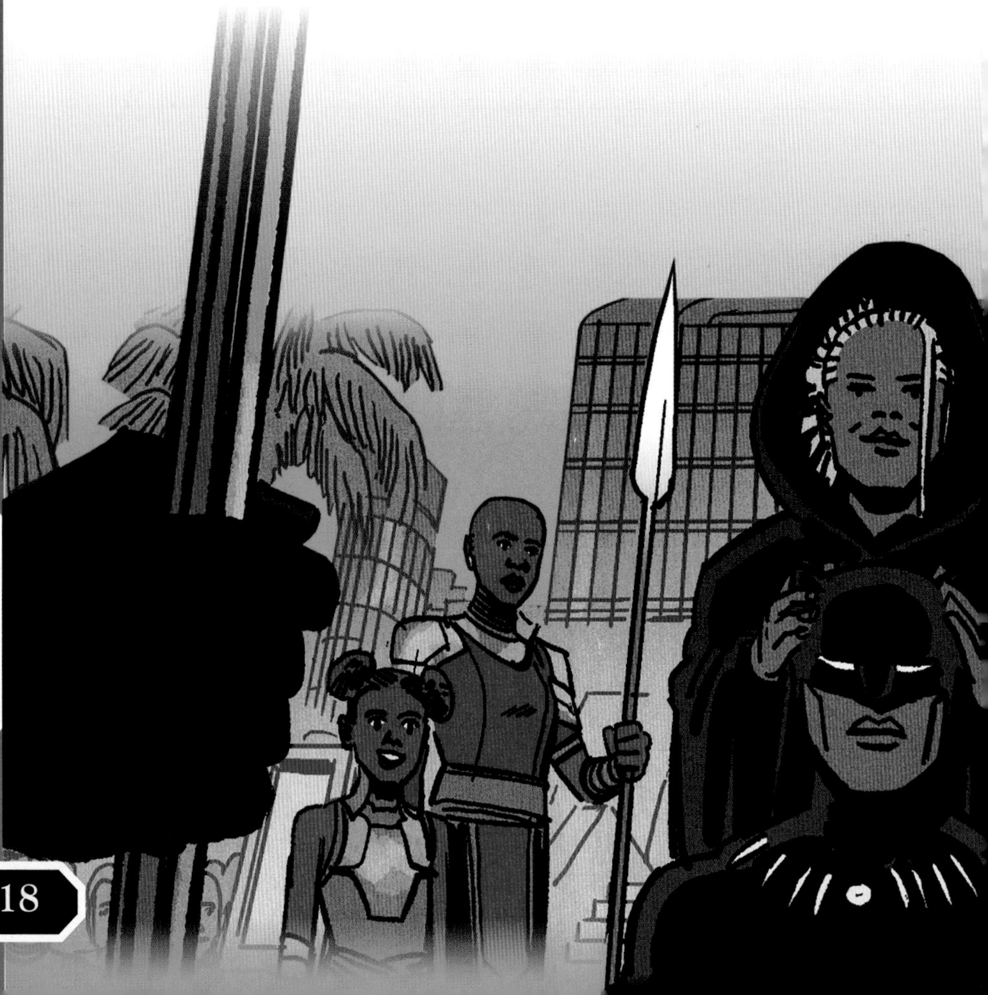

A person must go through tough trials before they are crowned Black Panther. Shuri will have to take the trials herself if T'Challa is injured. It would be a great honor to become the next protector of Wakanda!

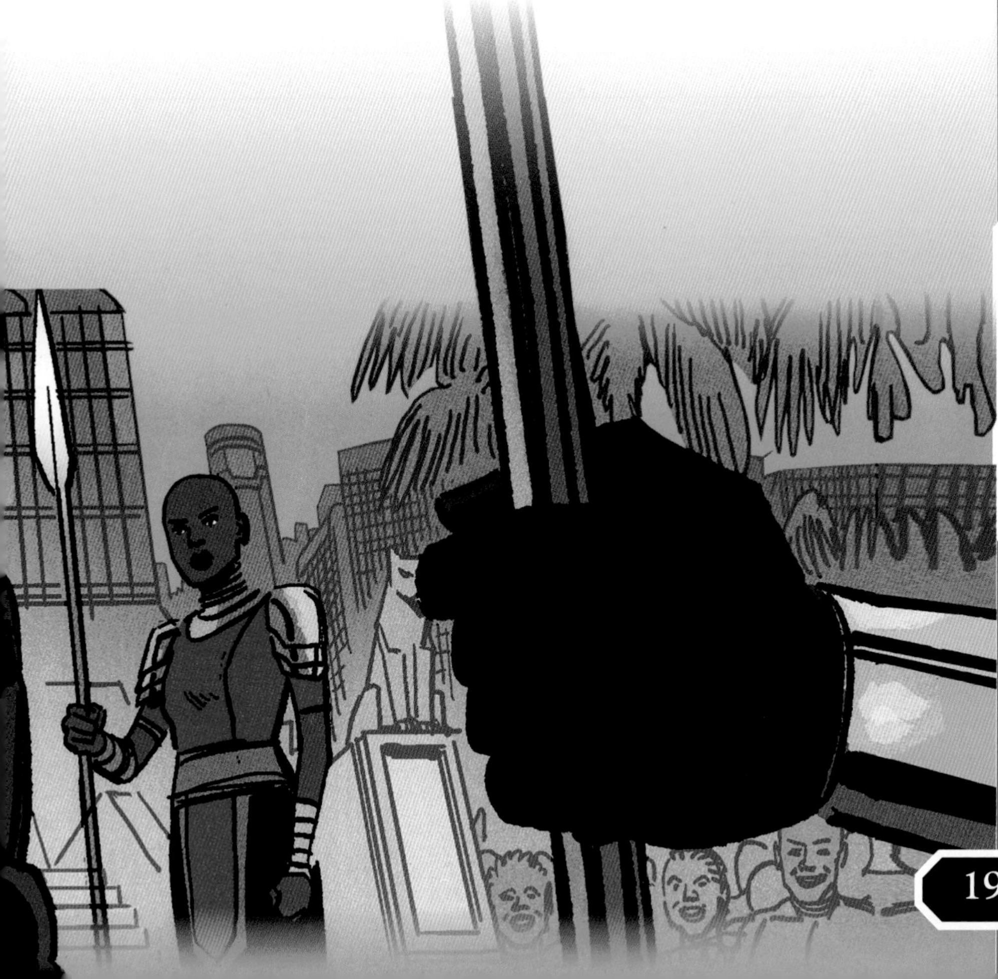

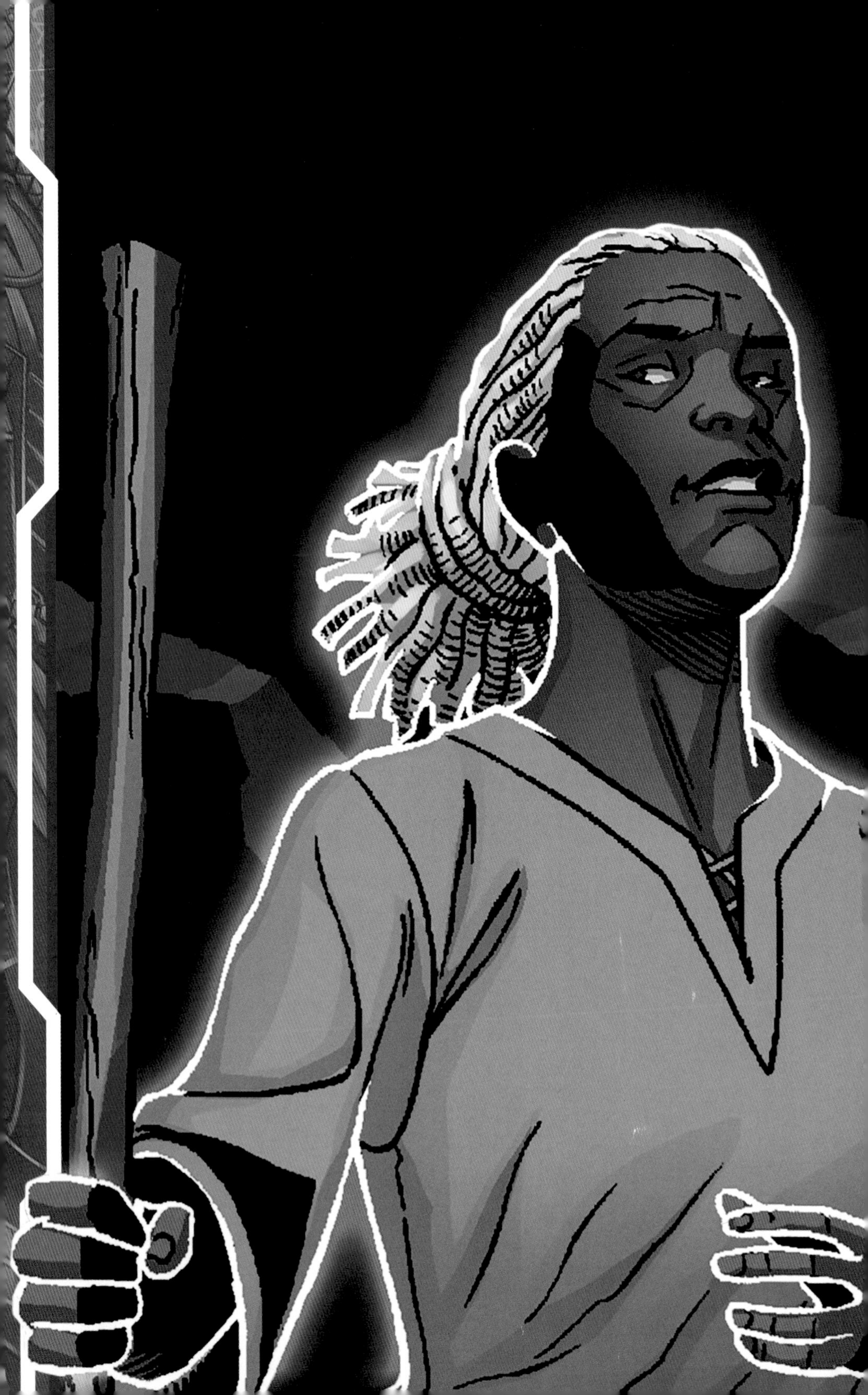

Queen Mother Ramonda

Ramonda is Shuri's mother and T'Challa's stepmother. She knows everything about Wakanda's important traditions. Ramonda will do whatever she can to stop anyone from discovering Wakanda's greatest secrets.

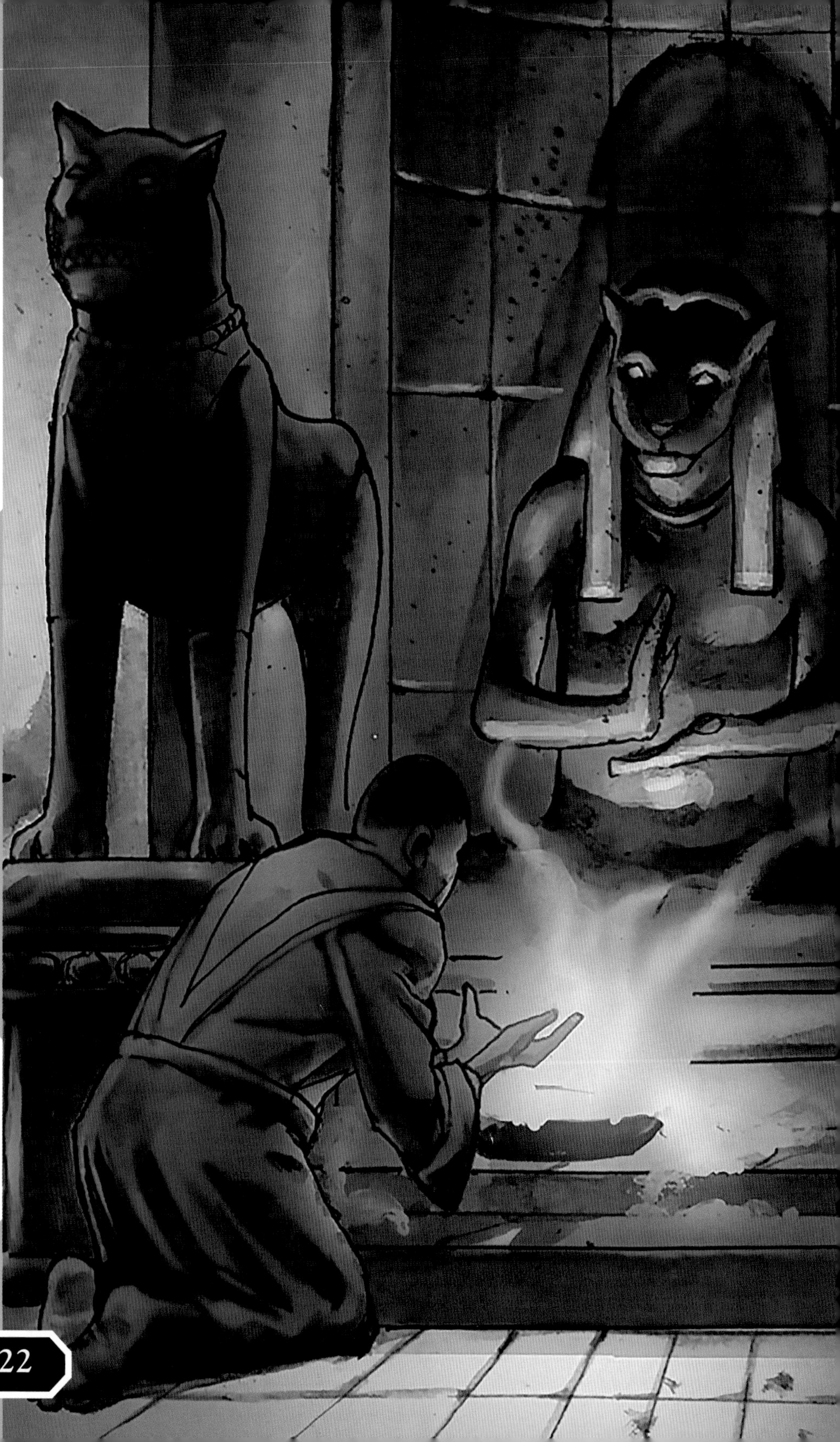

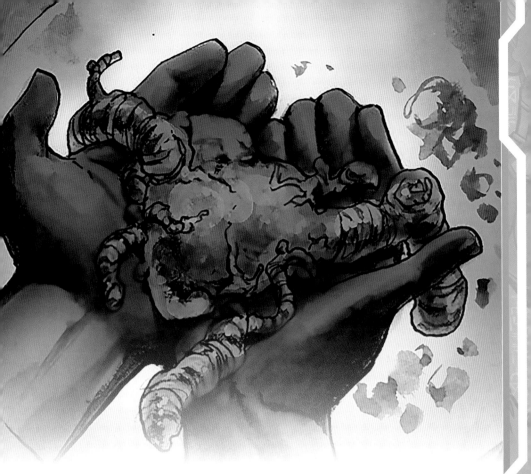

The heart-shaped herb

Black Panthers get their strength from a plant called the heart-shaped herb. A potion is made by crushing the herb. The potion gives Black Panther superhuman strength, speed, and stamina.

Dora Milaje

The Dora Milaje are a team of elite female soldiers. Their role is to protect and serve the Black Panther. The Dora Milaje are strong fighters with great combat skills. Shuri trains with the Dora Milaje to make sure she is always ready for battle.

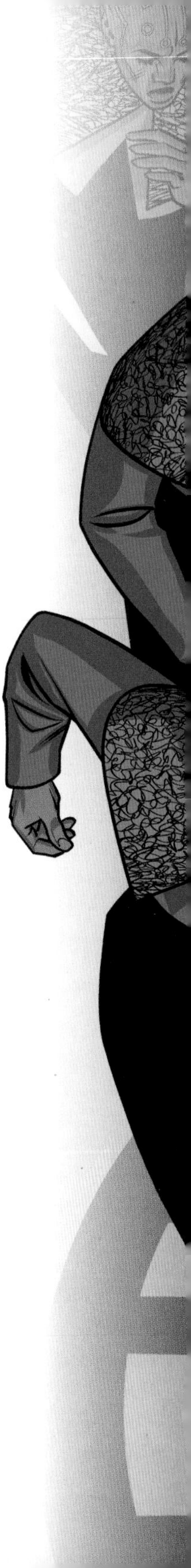

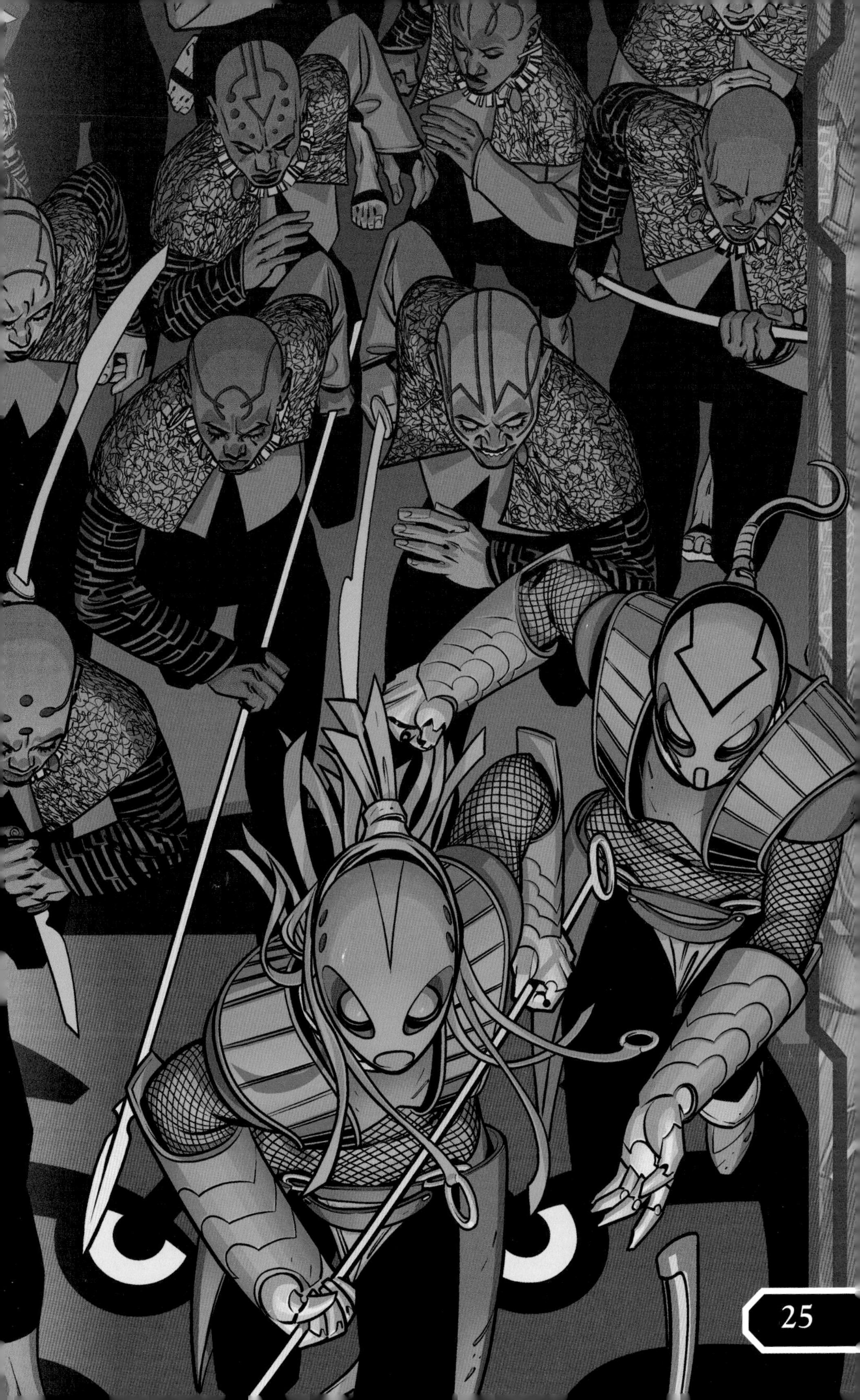

A new challenge

Shuri takes over as Black Panther when T'Challa is unable to fight. She leaves her work in the laboratory behind for a new challenge. She becomes the first female Black Panther: the protector of Wakanda!

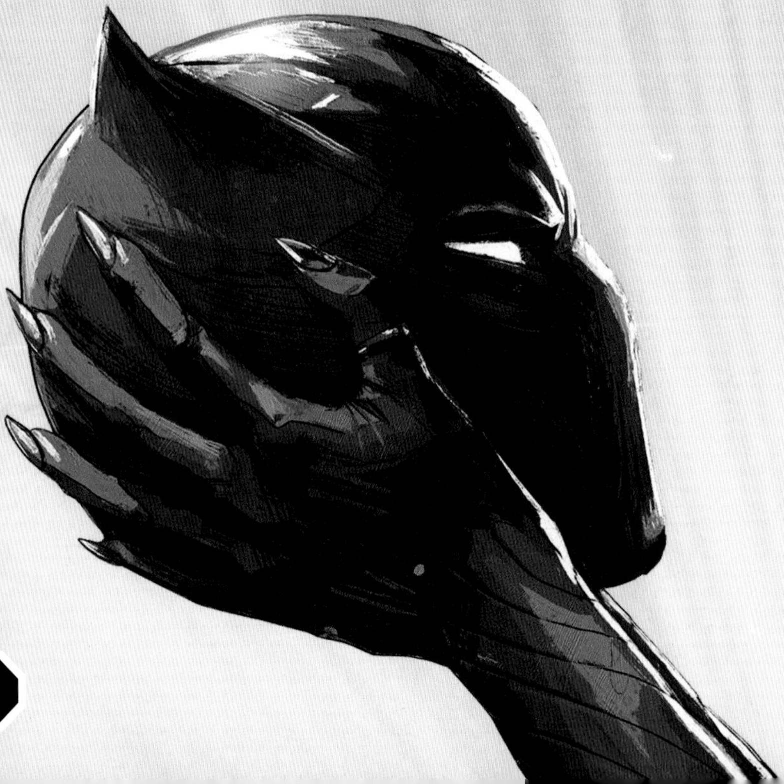

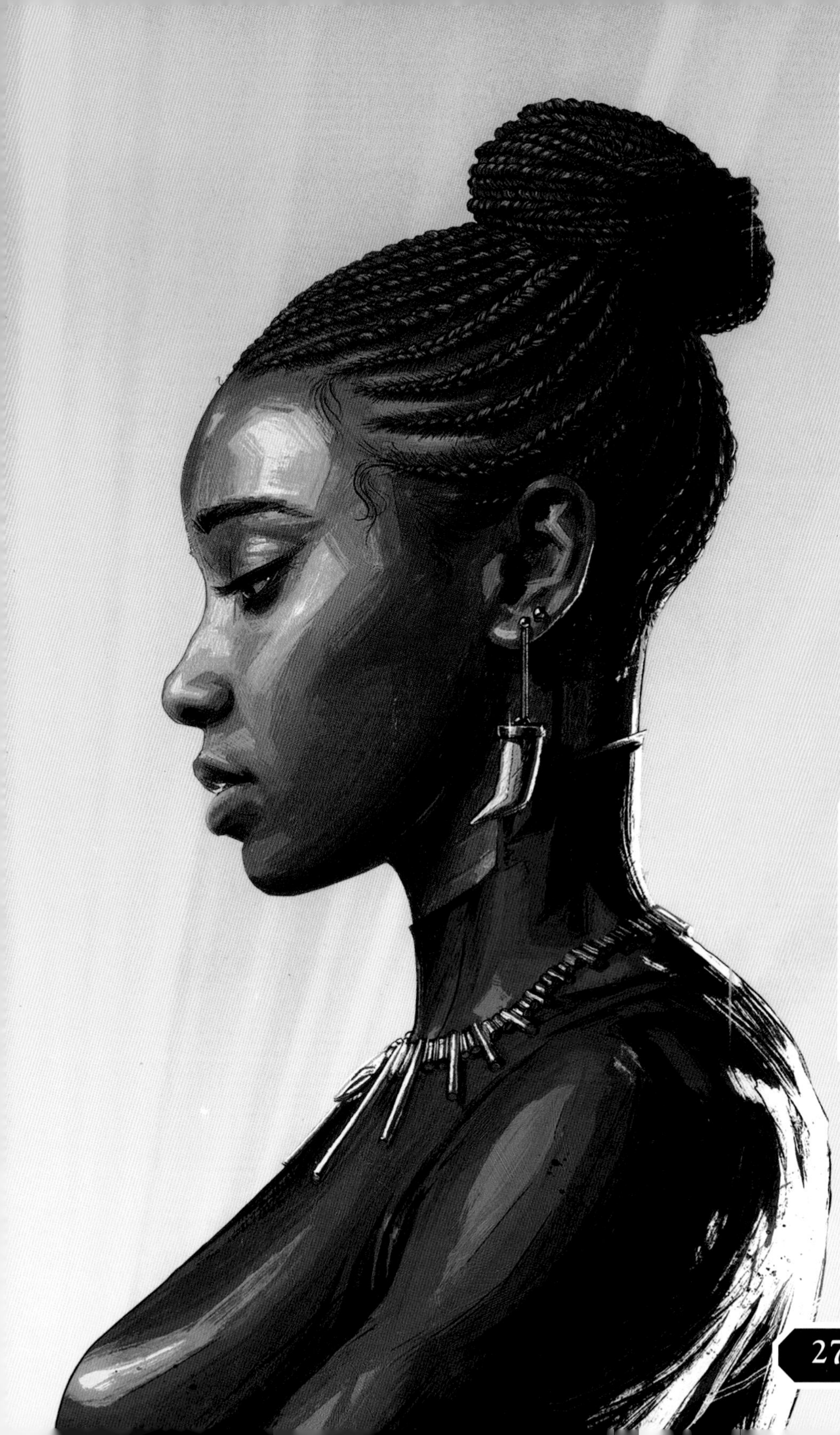

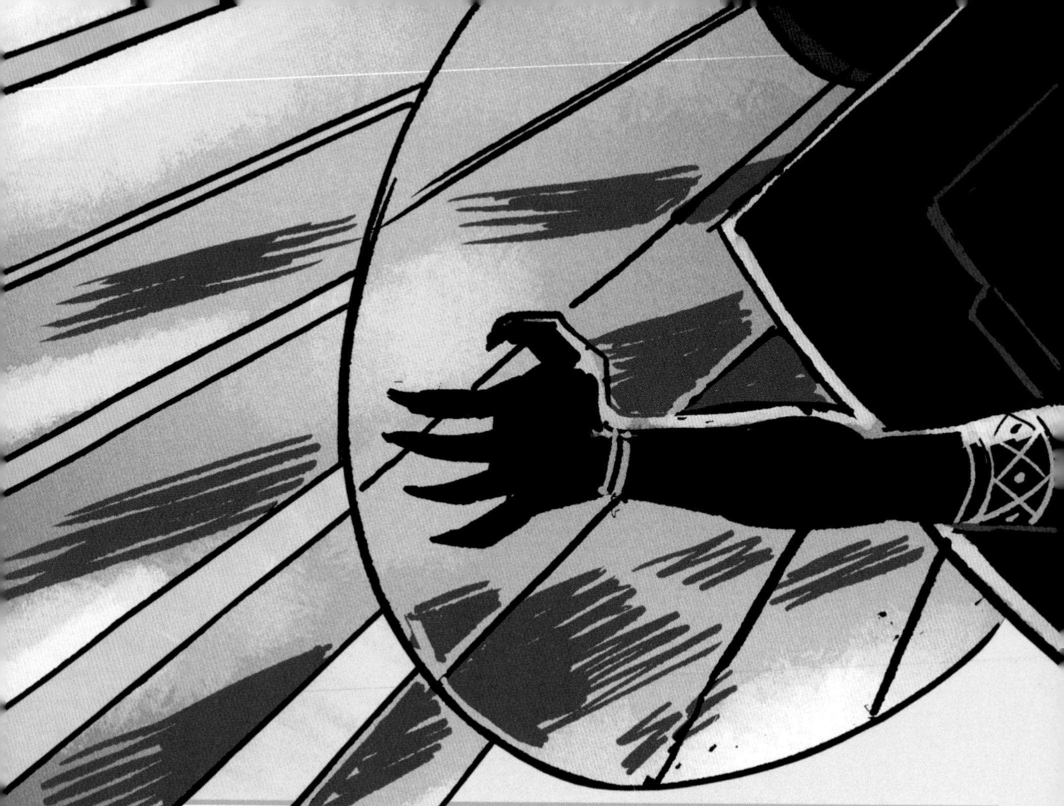

Shuri's Panther Habit

Shuri's special suit is called a Panther Habit. Shuri adds Vibranium wings to her habit, which allow her to glide and attack foes from above.

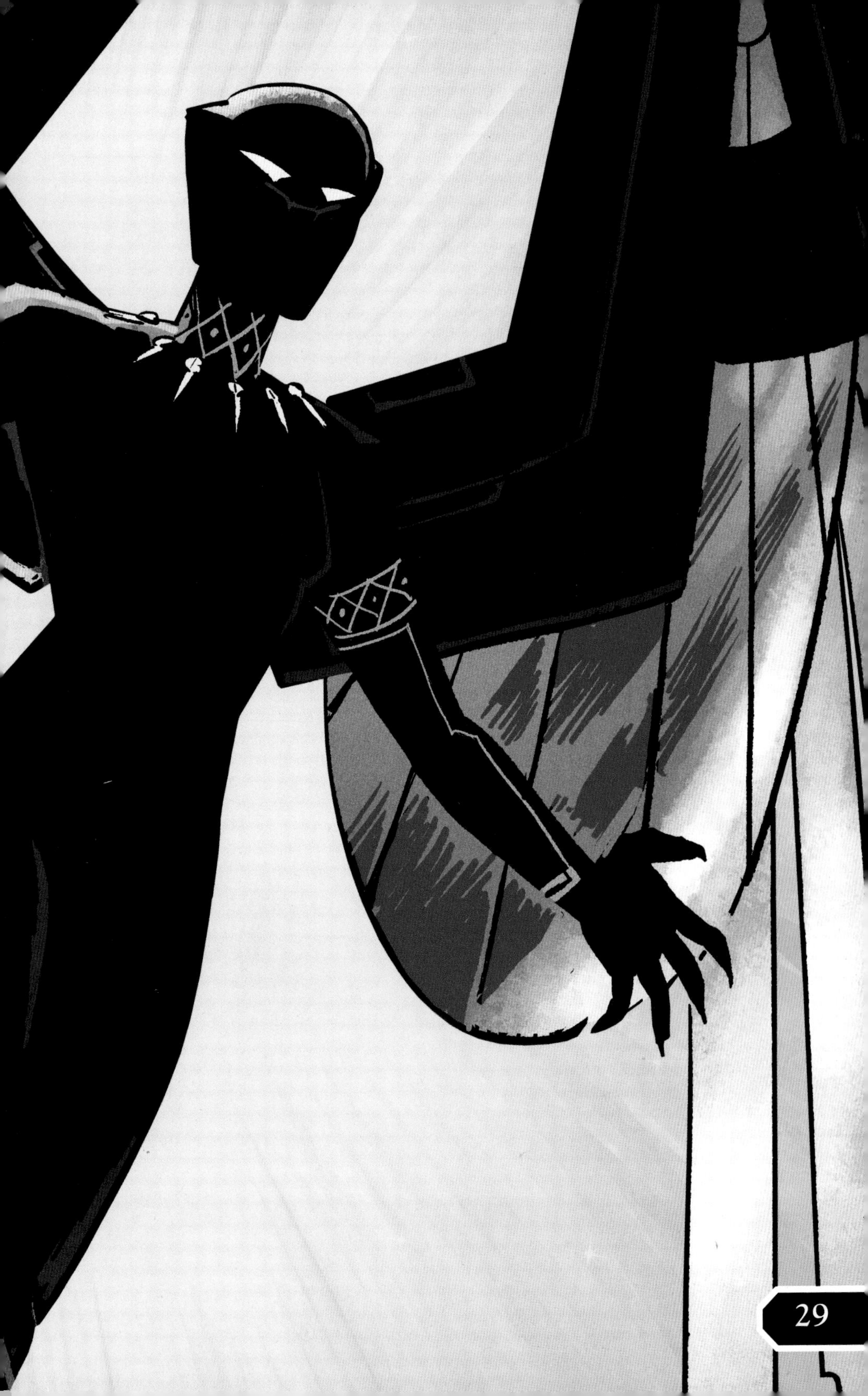

Iron Man

The Super Hero Iron Man joins Shuri in battle when aliens attack Wakanda. Iron Man loves technology just as much as Shuri does. They work together to defeat the aliens and save Wakanda.

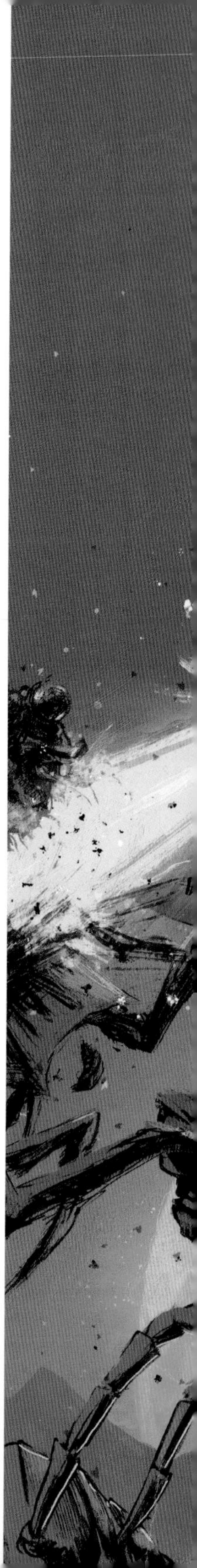

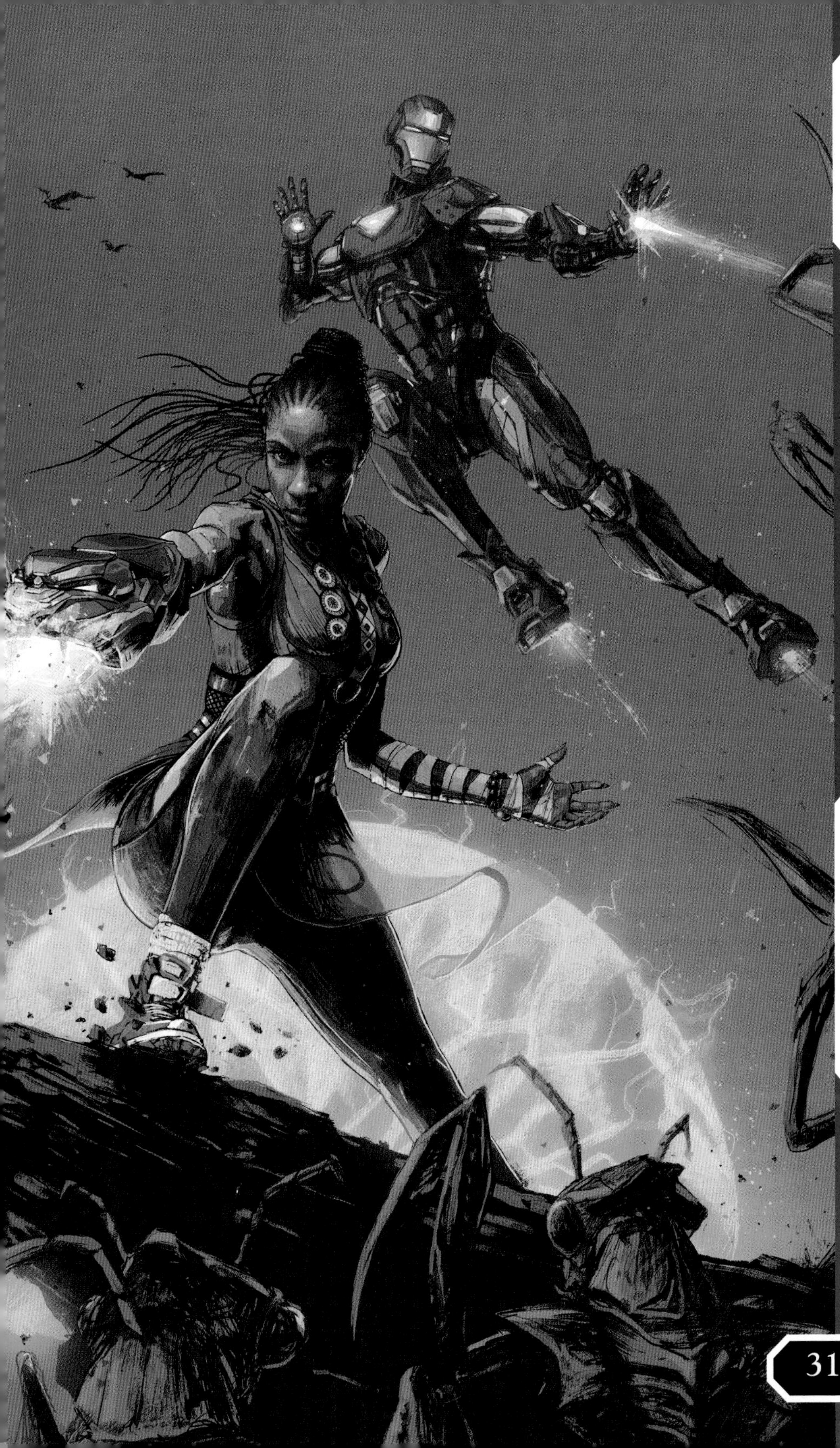

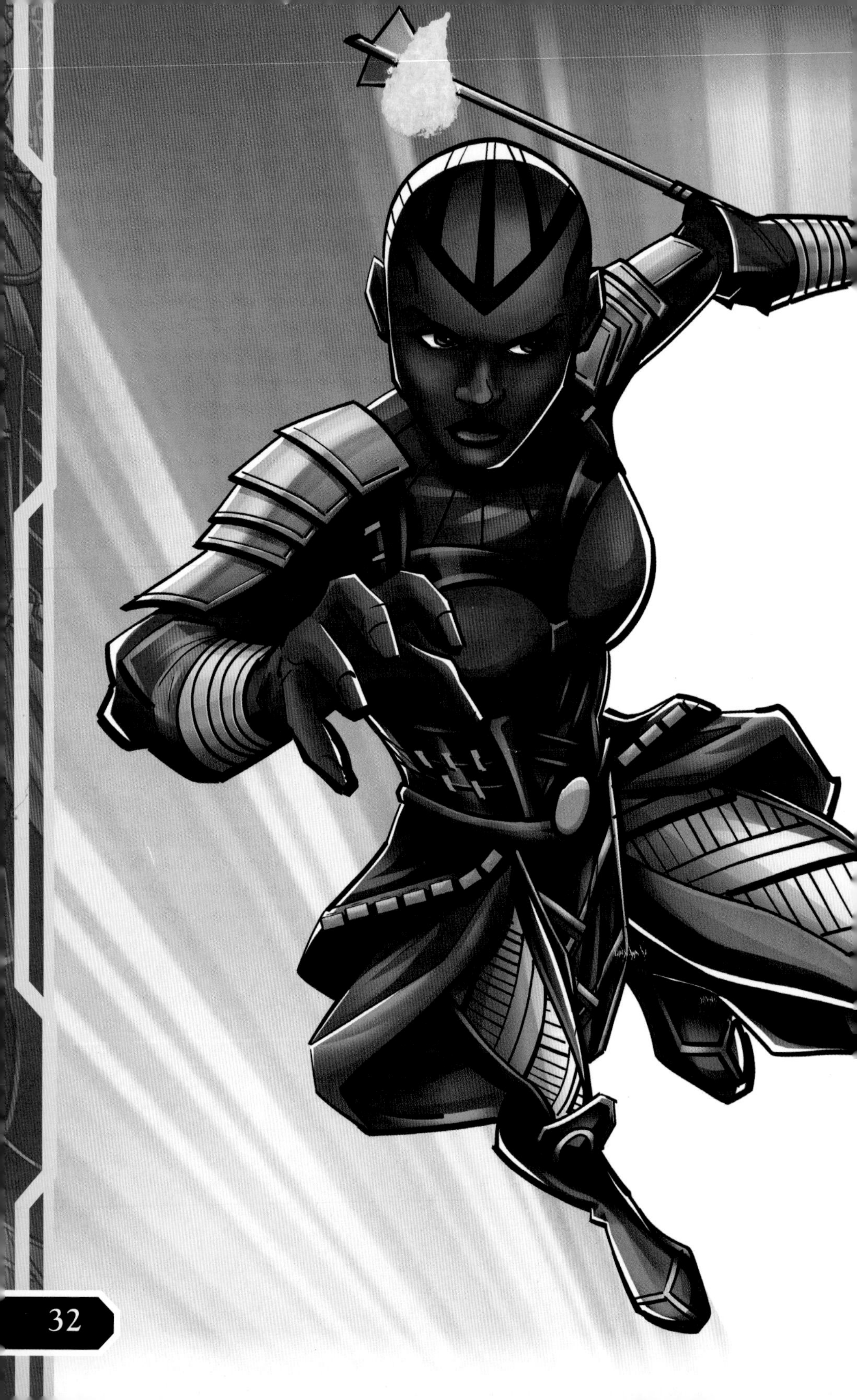

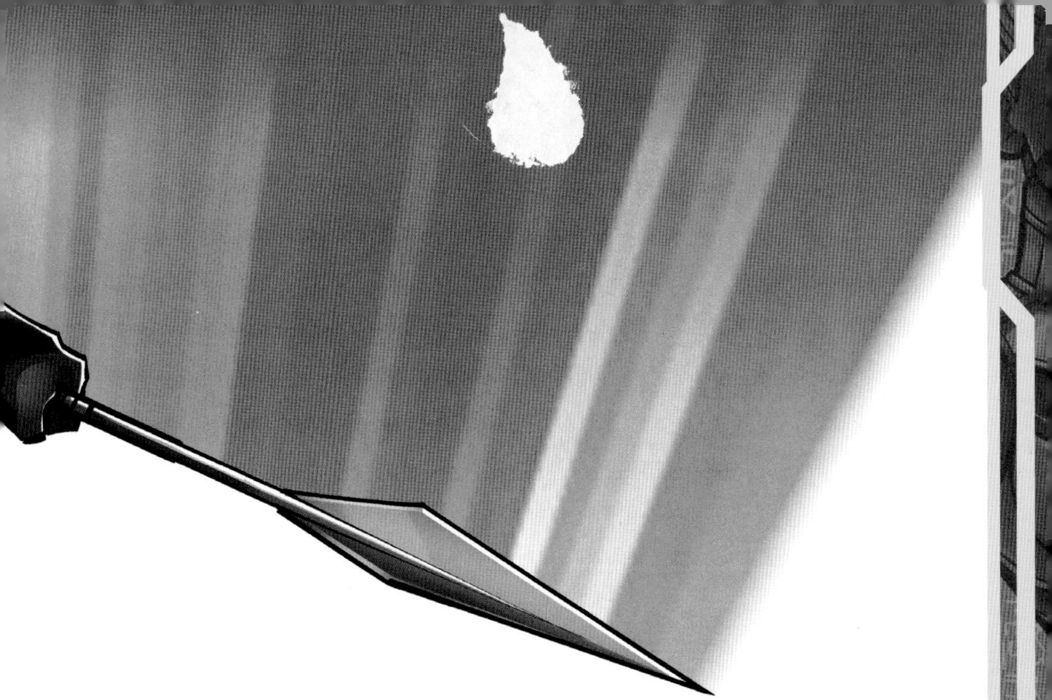

Okoye

General Okoye is the leader of the Dora Milaje. Okoye is a master of Wakandan martial arts. She is also very skilled at planning missions. She joins Black Panther on important operations. Okoye's favorite weapon is a Vibranium spear.

Thanos

Terrifying Thanos will do anything to get what he wants. He is the most dangerous villain in the universe. Thanos created powerful technology that he intends to use to rule over the galaxy. If he gains control, Wakanda will be destroyed. Can Shuri and Black Panther stop him?

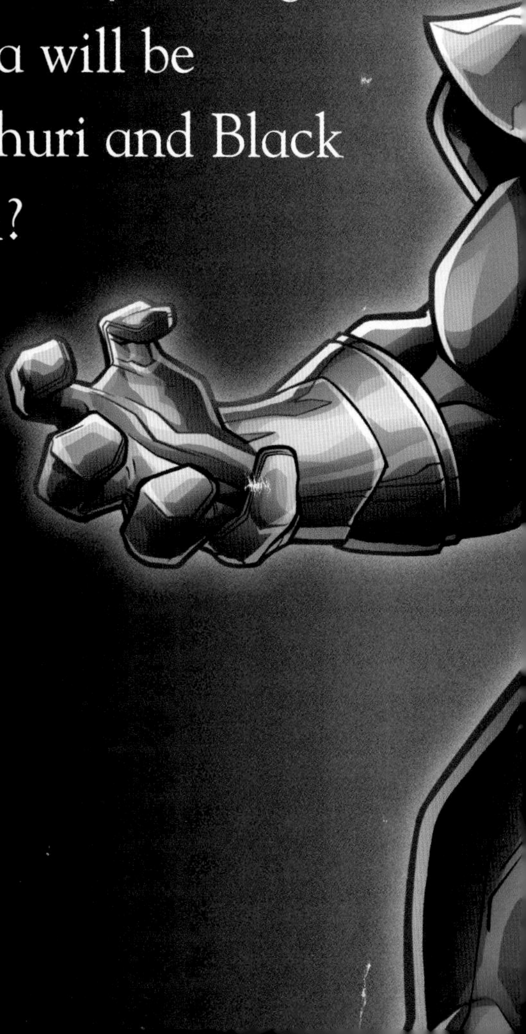

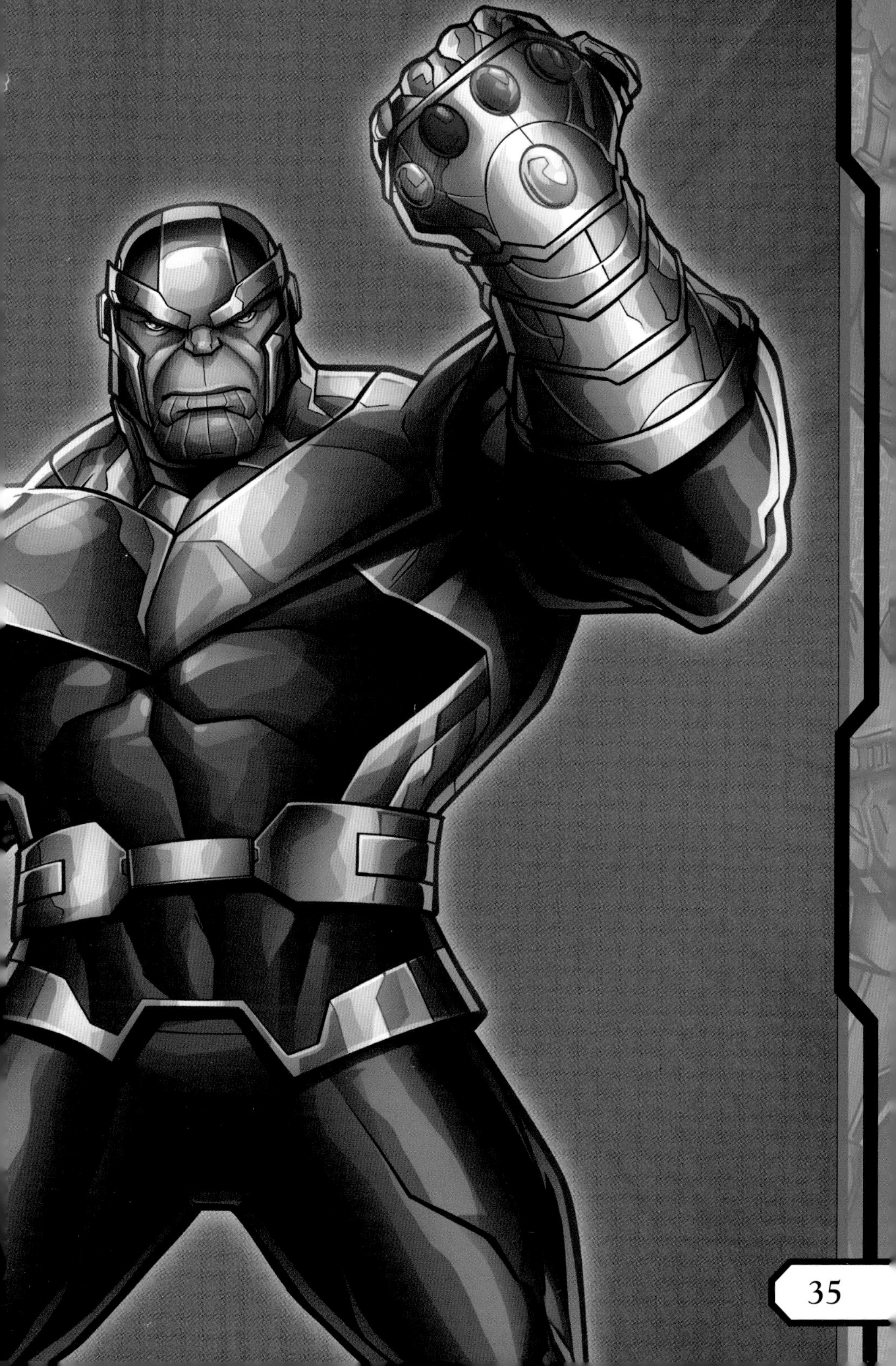

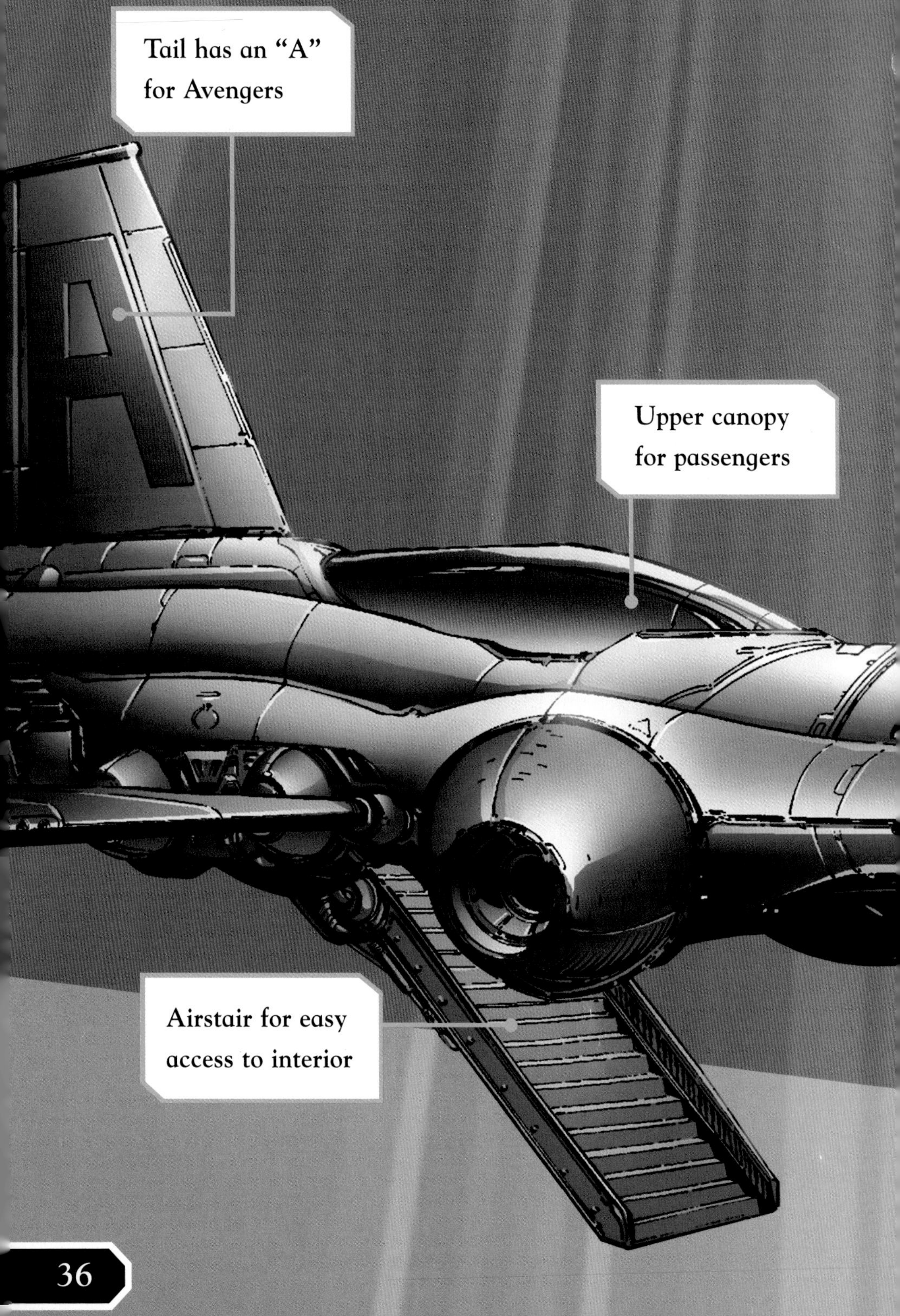
Tail has an "A" for Avengers
Upper canopy for passengers
Airstair for easy access to interior

Quinjet

The Quinjet was designed by Wakandan scientists. It is a high-tech flying machine that can reach amazing speeds. A team of Super Heroes called The Avengers use the Quinjet as their main form of transport.

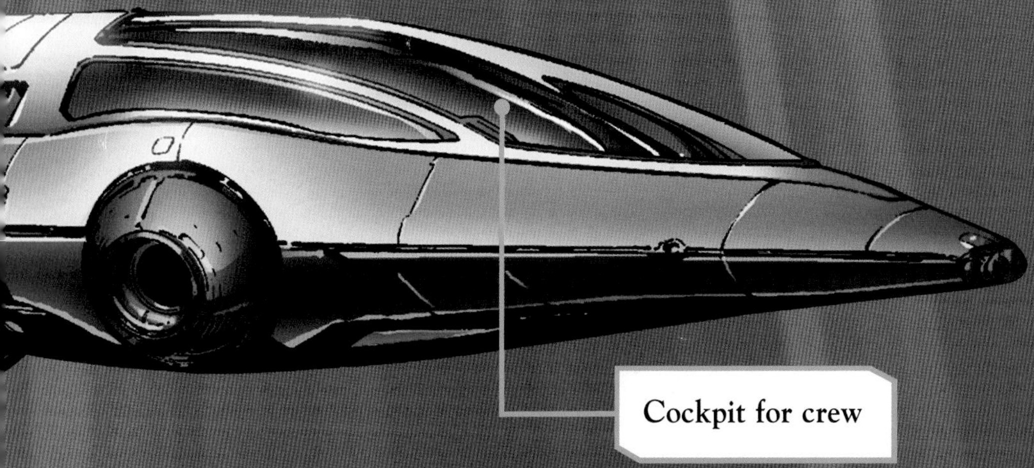
Cockpit for crew

Erik Killmonger

Erik Killmonger is from Wakanda, but he grew up in New York. He is extremely intelligent and strong. Erik has become one of Wakanda's biggest threats. He wants to destroy T'Challa and take the throne for himself.

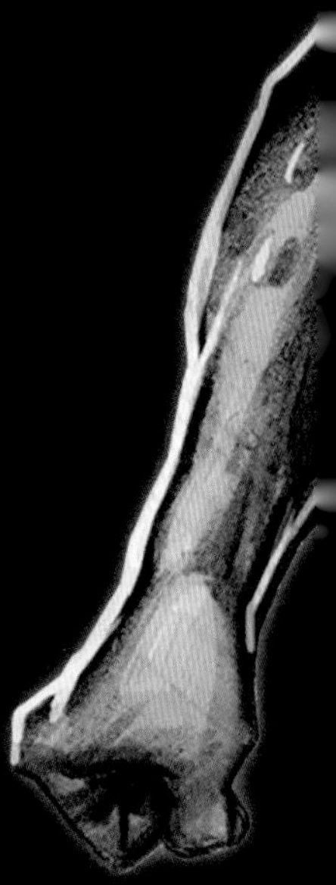

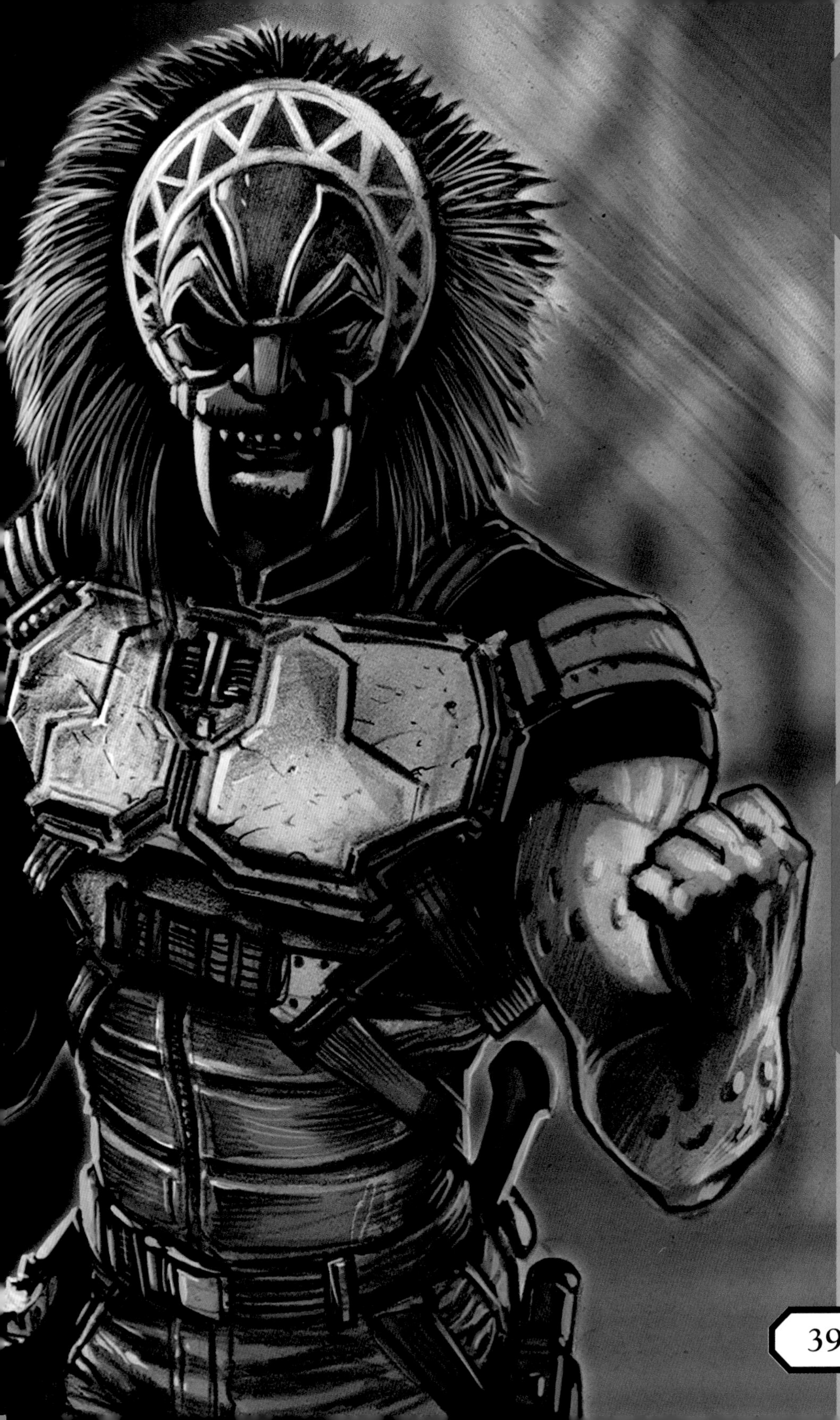

Vibranium gauntlets

Shuri is a fearsome fighter. She has been training for battle since she was a little girl. Shuri invented Vibranium gauntlets shaped like panthers that fire powerful bolts of energy. One blast from her gauntlets will knock anyone off their feet!

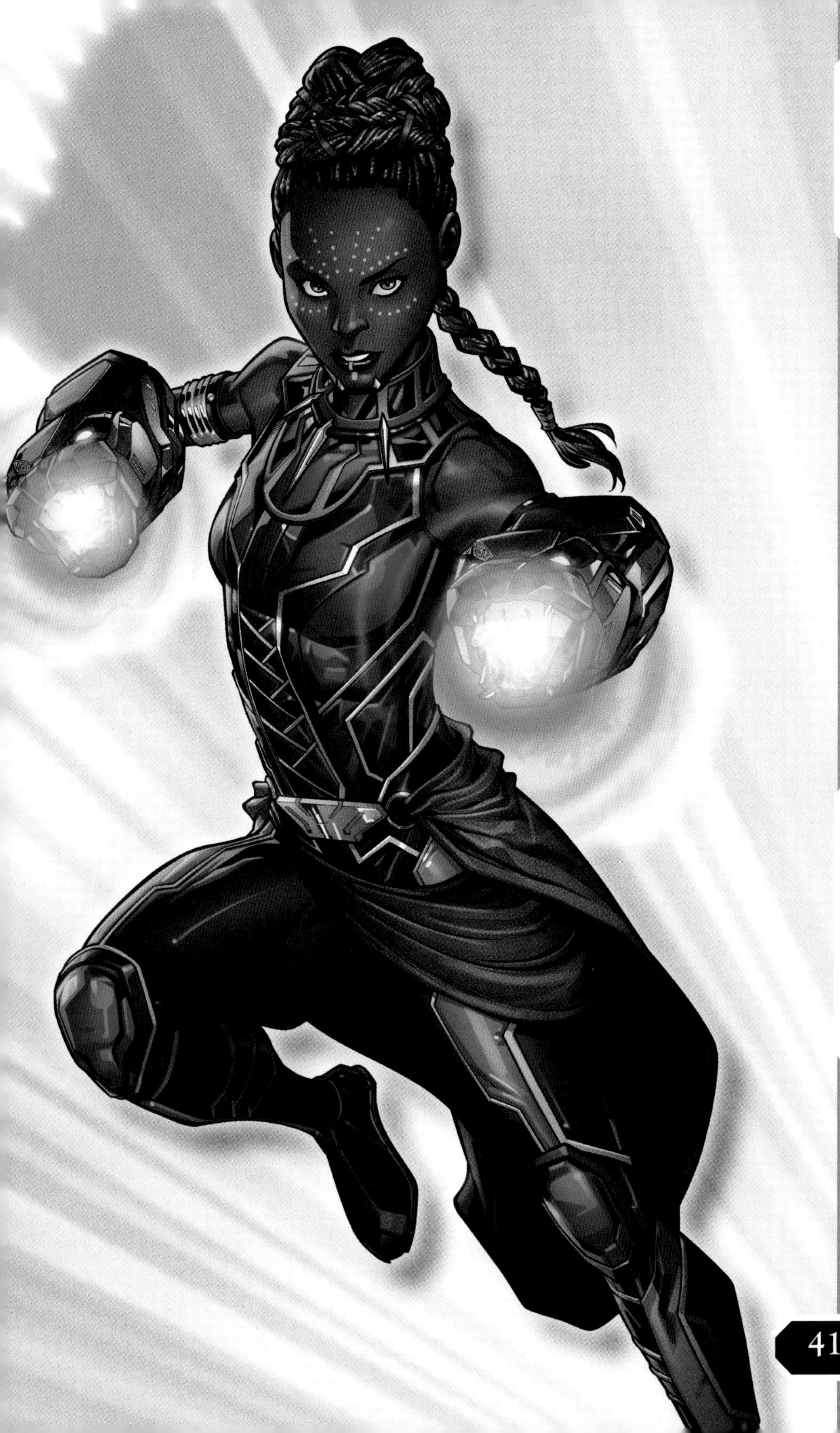

The perfect team

When Shuri and her brother work together, they are very hard to beat. They will always do whatever they can to make sure Wakanda and all of its amazing technology are safe!

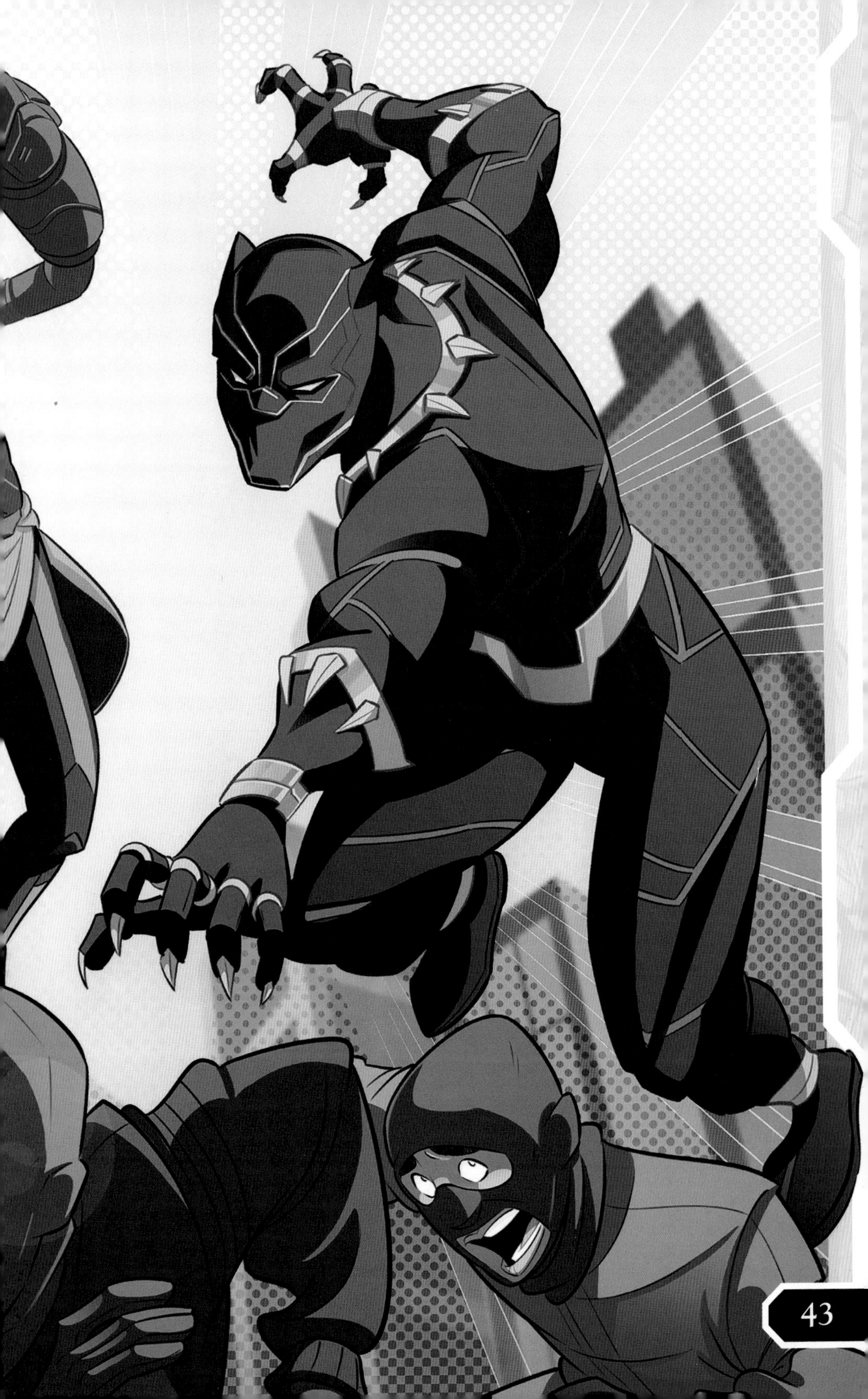

Quiz

1. How did Vibranium arrive in Wakanda?

2. What is Birnin Zana also called?

3. Who is Shuri's brother?

4. What herb gives Black Panthers their strength?

5. What is Shuri's special suit called?

6. Which Super Hero battles aliens with Shuri?

7. What makes Captain America's shield indestructible?

8. True or False? Shuri never trained with the Dora Milaje.

9. Who leads the Dora Milaje?

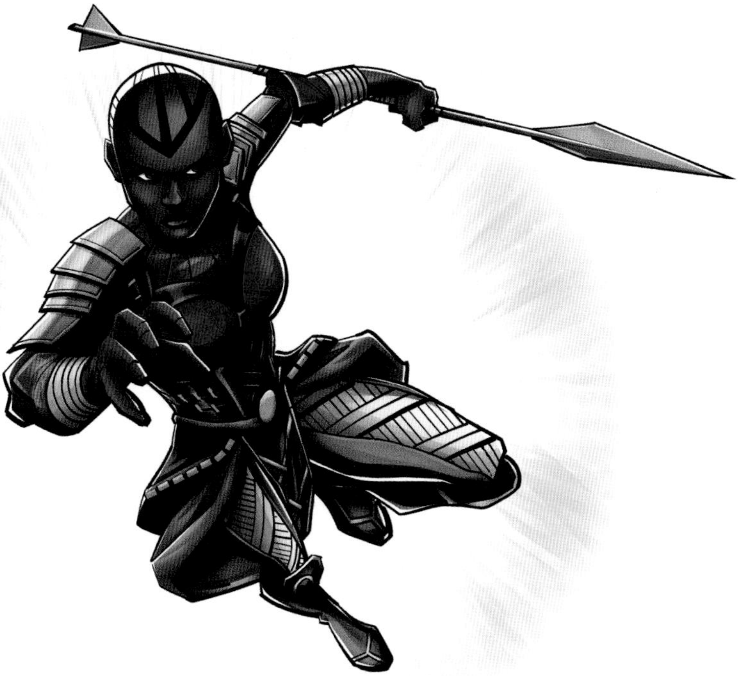

10. Who designed The Avengers's Quinjet?

Answers on page 47

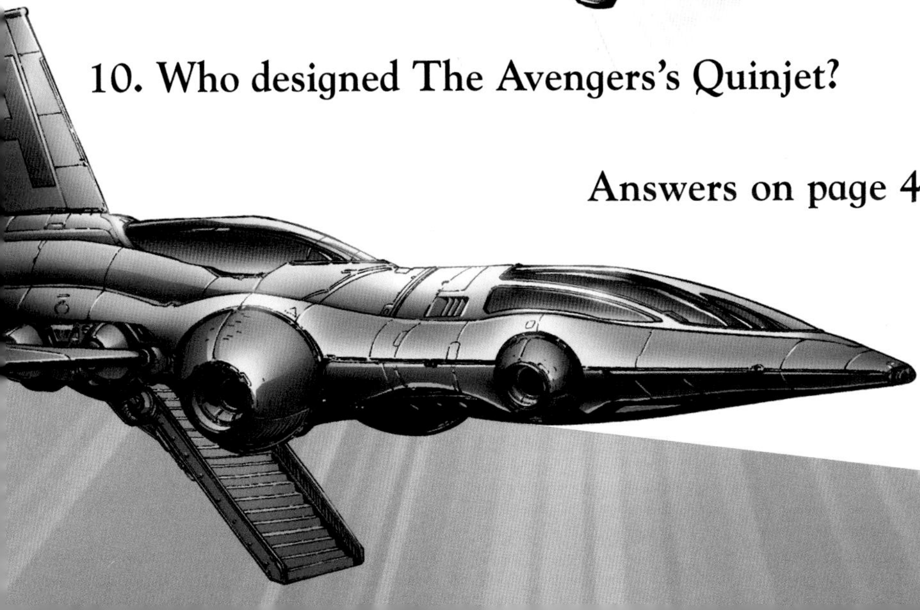

Glossary

technology
machines that help people with a task

traditions
beliefs or behaviors handed down over time

meteorite
a rock from space that has landed on earth

scientist
a person with great knowledge of science

inventing
creating, designing, or imagining something new

magnetic
able to pull or attract other metals

stamina
the ability to maintain physical strength for long
periods of time

laboratory
a room that is designed to help people conduct
experiments

Index

Answers to the quiz on pages 44 and 45
1. In a meteorite 2. The Golden City 3. T'Challa
4. The heart-shaped herb 5. A Panther Habit 6. Iron Man
7. Vibranium 8. False 9. Okoye 10. Wakandan scientists

A LEVEL FOR EVERY READER

This book is a part of an exciting four-level reading series to support children in developing the habit of reading widely for both pleasure and information. Each book is designed to develop a child's reading skills, fluency, grammar awareness, and comprehension in order to build confidence and enjoyment when reading.

Ready for a Level 2 (Beginning to Read) book

A child should:

- be able to recognize a bank of common words quickly and be able to blend sounds together to make some words.
- be familiar with using beginner letter sounds and context clues to figure out unfamiliar words.
- sometimes correct his/her reading if it doesn't look right or make sense.
- be aware of the need for a slight pause at commas and a longer one at periods.

A valuable and shared reading experience

For many children, reading requires much effort, but adult participation can make reading both fun and easier. Here are a few tips on how to use this book with a young reader:

Check out the contents together:

- read about the book on the back cover and talk about the contents page to help heighten interest and expectation.
- discuss new or difficult words.
- chat about labels, annotations, and pictures.

Support the reader:

- give the book to the young reader to turn the pages.
- where necessary, encourage longer words to be broken into syllables, sound out each one, and then flow the syllables together; ask him/her to reread the sentence to check the meaning.
- encourage the reader to vary her/his voice as she/he reads; demonstrate how to do this if helpful.

Talk at the end of each book, or after every few pages:

- ask questions about the text and the meaning of the words used—this helps develop comprehension skills.
- read the quiz at the end of the book and encourage the reader to answer the questions, if necessary, by turning back to the relevant pages to find the answers.

Reading consultant: Dr. Barbara Marinak, Dean and Professor of Education at Mount St. Mary's University, Maryland.

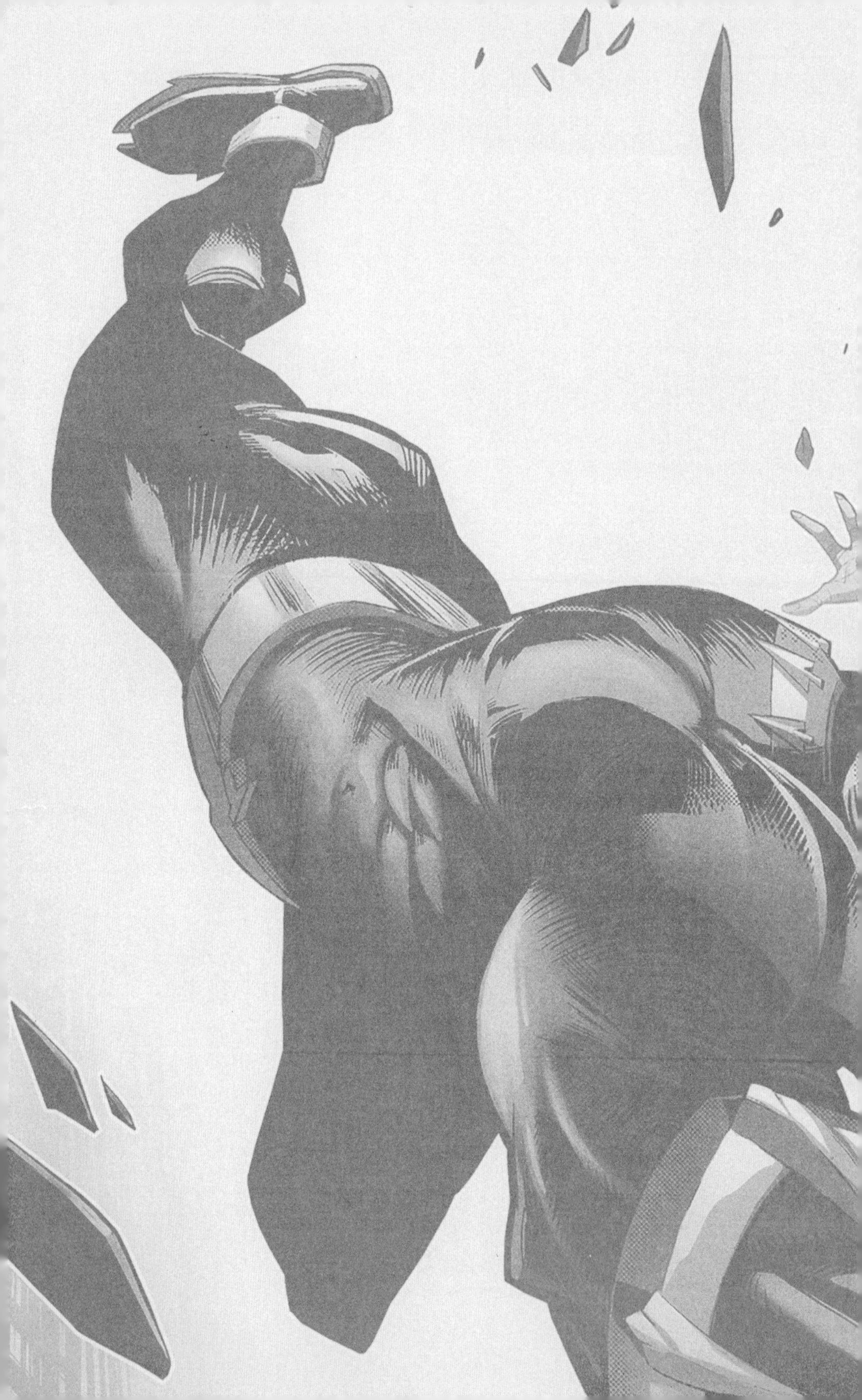